CULTURE SMART!

NORWAY

Linda March

Graphic Arts Books

First published in Great Britain 2006
by Kuperard, an imprint of Bravo Ltd.

Series Editor Geoffrey Chesler
Design DW Design

Simultaneously published in the U.S.A. and Canada
by Graphic Arts Center Publishing Company
P. O. Box 10306, Portland, OR 97296-0306

Library of Congress Cataloging-in-Publication Data

March, Linda Davis.
Norway : a quick guide to customs and etiquette / Linda March.
     p. cm. — (Culture smart!)
Includes bibliographical references and index.
ISBN-13: 978-1-55868-913-8 (softbound)
ISBN-10: 1-55868-913-3 (softbound)
1. Norway—Social life and customs—20th century.
2. Etiquette—Norway. 3. National characteristics, Norwegian.
4. Norway—Description and travel. I. Title. II. Series.
DL431.M37 2005
914.81—dc22

                                    2005019227

Printed in Malaysia

Cover image: Building on stilts, Lofoten Islands.
Travel Ink/Roy Westlake

CultureSmart!Consulting and **Culture Smart!** guides both contribute
to and regularly feature in the weekly travel program "Fast Track" on
BBC World TV.

About the Author

LINDA MARCH is a writer with a special interest in issues affecting expatriate families. Born in Edinburgh, Scotland, into a Royal Navy family, she has spent much of her life on the move, living and working in Europe and the U.S.A. A graduate of Hull University, she is a former head teacher and has also worked in the computer industry as a programmer and trainer. Linda lived in Stavanger, Norway, for six years, during which time she was on the Board of the Women's International Network (WIN).

Other Books in the Series

- Culture Smart! Argentina
- Culture Smart! Australia
- Culture Smart! Belgium
- Culture Smart! Brazil
- Culture Smart! Britain
- Culture Smart! Costa Rica
- Culture Smart! China
- Culture Smart! Czech Republic
- Culture Smart! Denmark
- Culture Smart! Finland
- Culture Smart! France
- Culture Smart! Germany
- Culture Smart! Greece
- Culture Smart! Hong Kong
- Culture Smart! India
- Culture Smart! Ireland
- Culture Smart! Italy
- Culture Smart! Japan
- Culture Smart! Korea
- Culture Smart! Mexico
- Culture Smart! Netherlands
- Culture Smart! Philippines
- Culture Smart! Poland
- Culture Smart! Portugal
- Culture Smart! Russia
- Culture Smart! Singapore
- Culture Smart! Spain
- Culture Smart! Sweden
- Culture Smart! Switzerland
- Culture Smart! Thailand
- Culture Smart! Turkey
- Culture Smart! Ukraine
- Culture Smart! USA
- Culture Smart! Vietnam

Other titles are in preparation. For more information, contact: info@kuperard.co.uk

The publishers would like to thank **CultureSmart!**Consulting for its help in researching and developing the concept for this series.

contents

contents

Map of Norway

introduction

Norway is breathtakingly beautiful. From its rugged coastline, where fjords have carved their way into the land, to its wild mountainous backbone, from its arctic tundra to the golden sands of its unspoiled southern beaches, it offers a wide range of physical contrasts. To get the most from your visit to the Land of the Midnight Sun, however, it helps to have some background knowledge of what makes the people of this northern kingdom tick. *Culture Smart! Norway* aims to take you past their reserved exterior to an understanding of how the terrain and climate have shaped the Norwegian people. As well as an insight into their values and attitudes, it provides a useful outline of how the Norwegian commercial world operates—vital information for anyone doing business with one of the world's wealthiest nations.

And for when the working day is over, this book provides tips on meeting and communicating with "real" Norwegians that will make socializing a pleasant and comfortable experience. Chapters on the customs and traditions that form the bedrock of family life will open the door to a glimpse of life inside a Norwegian home. Understanding the behavior appreciated by your hosts will enable you to accept an invitation from your new Norwegian friends without apprehension.

Norway is a rich nation whose inhabitants enjoy arguably the best quality of life in the world. With no real poverty, a welfare state that provides for the basic needs of all, and a strong commitment to equality and fairness, Norwegians are naturally proud of the society they have created and see themselves as the equals of anyone. A deep respect for the wildness and beauty of the natural world is ingrained in the national character of a people who delight in the great outdoors.

On first encounter, Norwegians are serious, polite, law-abiding, and very hardy. They are also very private people, which can make the newcomer feel as if they have come up against a stone wall with an icy wind blowing behind it. Getting to know a Norwegian takes time, but when you are able to read the signs that take you behind that façade you will meet the warm, friendly, fun-loving, family-oriented person hiding on the other side.

Culture Smart! Norway can help steer you through the social and professional encounters of your visit to this new culture, deepening your understanding, and enabling you to establish business partnerships and friendships with ease.

Key Facts

Official Name	Kingdom of Norway (*Kongeriket Norge*)	
Capital City	Oslo	
Main Towns	Bergen, Trondheim, Stavanger, Tromsø, Kristiansand	Tromsø is the world's most northerly cathedral and university town.
Area	150,000 sq. miles (386,958 sq. km)	65% mountainous. Less than 5% of land is cultivated.
Climate	Long, very cold winters in north, temperate on coast, cooler inland	Up to 80 in (2032 mm) rain per year in west, less than 30 in (800 mm) in east
Currency	Norwegian *krone* (pl. *kroner*). In 2005 NKr 6.4 = U.S. $1 NKr 11.9 = £1	
Population	4.5 million	Average life expectancy: 77 for men, 82 for women
Ethnic Makeup	93% Norwegians 7% others	The Sami (Lapps) are the indigenous population (approx. 20,000).
Family Makeup	Av. no. of children per family is 2.	50% of marriages end in divorce.
Language	Norwegian (Bokmål and Nynorsk), Sami	English compulsory from age 6. Third language often French or German
Religion	Official Protestant state Church	Church of Norway (Evangelical Lutheran) 88%, Islam 60,000, Pentecostal 45,000, Roman Catholic 40,000, Jewish 1,000

Government	Constitutional monarchy, parliamentary democracy	Monarch has no political power. Parliament (the *Storting*) has 165 members. Elections every 4 years
Media	The Norwegian Broadcasting Corporation (NRK) runs 2 public service TV channels: NRK1 and NRK2, and 3 radio channels. Two commercial channels: TV Norge and TV2. Commercial radio stations. Cable and satellite channels	The largest-circulation national newspapers are *Aftenposten, Verdens Gang*, and *Dagbladet*. The west coast has *Bergens Tidende* and *Stavanger Aftenbladet*. *Dagens Næringsliv* is the principal business paper.
Media: English Language	Many TV programs are imported from the English-speaking world and rarely dubbed. English language cable channels	The NATO radio station broadcasts in English.
Electricity	220 volts, 50 Hz	Plugs are two-pronged.
TV / Video / DVD	PAL system, DVD Europe Region 2	Incompatible with U.S. systems
Telephone	Norway's country code is 47. To dial out of Norway dial 00, then the code of the country required.	One of the most advanced telecommunications networks in Europe.
Time Zone	UK GMT + 1 USA EST + 6	DST+1 last Sunday in March – last Sunday in October

LAND &
PEOPLE

Think of Norway and what springs to mind?
Fjords, snowy rugged mountains, the Land of the
Midnight Sun, maybe oil too? Not surprisingly, the
features that have impressed themselves on the
minds of outsiders are those that have shaped the
Norwegian people: the geography and the climate.

Only 4.5 million people inhabit a country
approximately the size of California or the United
Kingdom and 70 percent of them live in or
around a handful of urban communities. This
leaves most of this long, spoon-shaped country
very sparsely populated and there is certainly
plenty of the great outdoors to satisfy the national
passion for fresh air and freedom.

And what of the Norwegian people: the blond,
blue-eyed Nordic majority and the short, dark
Sami of the north? We might be surprised to find
that the fair-haired descendants of marauding
Vikings are a mild mannered, modest people who
have quietly created a wealthy nation and a
society with highly civilized values.

Too small to be a major player in world affairs,

Norway is a land that knows its own mind and is happy to work behind the scenes to broker peace and influence others by the example of its fairness and generosity.

GEOGRAPHY

With Russia and Finland as its northern neighbors in the Arctic Circle, Norway shares a 1,000-mile (1,600 km) eastern border with Sweden to form the long thin landmass (in places less than 5 miles, or 8 km, wide) of the Scandinavian peninsula that juts down toward Denmark in the south.

But it is the west coast that gives Norway its character. The country runs over 1,000 miles (1,600 km) in length  from the Arctic North Cape to the sunny resort of Kristiansand in the south. But the jagged indentations of its west coast fjords, the remote Svalbard (Spitsbergen) archipelago 400 miles (640 km) north of the mainland, and numerous small islands give it a coastline of over 13,700 miles (21,900 km). No wonder the sea has played such a large part in Norwegian life over the centuries, from Viking exploration, to fishing and shipbuilding, to the "messing about in boats" of today's leisure and tourism.

Occupying a total of 150,000 sq. miles (386,958 sq. km), Norway is Europe's sixth-largest country in terms of its landmass. However, statistics such as one-third of the land inside the Arctic Circle and two-thirds mountainous mean that only a small percentage of land is suitable for productive agriculture or forestry, much of that in the south and west. Inland farms grew up in remote valleys and as a result isolation has been a major feature of Norwegian life over the centuries. In a country divided by a backbone of mountains and

fjords, transportation and communication have traditionally presented problems that the twenty-first century is beginning to solve. Nevertheless, large areas, particularly in the north and east, are unpopulated, leaving Norway to rank only twenty-eighth in Europe in terms of population.

CLIMATE

Many expect the climate of a country sharing the same latitude as Alaska, Siberia, and Greenland to be harsh and cold. This is undoubtedly a true picture in some areas of Norway at some times, but considering the country's extreme northern position, its climate is surprisingly mild and varied. This is largely due to the warm and steady current of the Gulf Stream off its west coast, which means that even areas inside the Arctic Circle enjoy winter temperatures well above those normally expected at a similar latitude.

The amount of sunlight received during the year also varies. In northern Norway the summer months are brief, but the effects of the Midnight Sun mean that summers are bright and warm, sometimes even registering temperatures of 86°F (30°C). For most of the country the winters are snowy and dark. Those on the southwest coast, for whom the winter precipitation is more often rain, enjoy the occasional periods of snow and the brightness they bring.

Norway's west coast often knows a battering from high winds. Rainfall of up to 80 inches (2,032 mm) is found annually here, along with cool summers and mild winters. Bergen residents experience over two hundred rainy days per year.

The high mountain ranges that divide Norway provide protection for large eastern and inland areas, where rainfall may be less than 12 inches (300 mm) per year. Although winters are cold, summers are warm and generally dry, allowing the Continental feel of pavement café dining in summertime Oslo.

No matter where in Norway, the winter is long, dark, and bleak, which undoubtedly has a depressing effect on its people. Winter is for hibernating beside comforting wood fires. The summer is unquestioningly spent outdoors and Norway comes to life. No scrap of sunshine is wasted. The first bright March day will find Norwegians reclining on their decks and patios, wrapped in blankets against the cold, but making the most of the first hint of spring.

Average Temperatures

	January	July
Oslo	25°F / -3.9°C	65°F / 18.3°C
Bergen	35°F / 1.6°C	58°F / 14.5°C
Trondheim	26°F / -3.3°C	59°F / 15.0°C
Tromsø	23°F / -5.0°C	53.2°F / 11.8°C

Average Rainfall

	January	July
Oslo	2.3 in / 58.1 mm	3.3 in / 84.7 mm
Bergen	7.6 in / 193 mm	5.5 in / 139 mm
Trondheim	2.8 in / 72.3 mm	2.7 in / 68.3 mm
Tromsø	4.1 in / 104.3 mm	2.7 in / 68.3 mm

The Land of the Midnight Sun
Seeing the Midnight Sun is popular with many of Norway's summer visitors and involves a trip into

the Arctic Circle. This invisible line is the southernmost point at which the sun shines for twenty-four hours without setting, for at least one day of the year. The Midnight Sun can be seen from mid-May to late July. The further north you go, the longer the duration. An amazing spectacle, it does present sleeping problems for many Norwegians. Its downside occurs in the winter months when the Arctic Circle pays for all this daylight with twenty-four-hour darkness.

Average Hours of Daylight		
	January	**July**
Oslo	6 hours 3 mins	18 hours 41 mins
Trondheim	4 hours 44 mins	20 hours 21 mins
Tromsø	none	24 hours

The Northern Lights

Also known as the Aurora Borealis, this amazing natural phenomenon, which blazes a dramatic arc of colored lights across the night sky, is well worth a visit to the north of Norway. Seen in polar regions, the lights occur when electrically charged solar particles enter the earth's atmosphere at tremendous speed and collide with the highest air particles. The air then lights up, its colors reflecting the gases. The Northern Lights are most

visible on clear nights between November and
March in Tromsø and Finnmark.

A BRIEF HISTORY
The Viking Era

The first Norwegians were nomadic hunters who
followed the seasonal migrations of reindeer

herds around 11,000
BCE. Some 5,000 years
later, permanent
settlement began.
Around 500 BCE a
deteriorating climate
resulted in Norway's

previously nomadic population settling into
farming communities. By the mid-eighth century
it had developed into a nation of small,
independent Gothic kingdoms, separated from
each other by the mountainous terrain. The first
successful attempt to unite these kingdoms was
made around 885 CE by Harald Hårfagre (Harald
the Fairhaired) who could be said to be Norway's
first king. The union was dissolved after his death.

As today, the sea played an important role in
the life of early Norwegians and led to a long
tradition of seafaring and shipbuilding. Large
rowing boats enabled them to exploit the coastal
waters, but by the eighth century Scandinavians

had perfected the seagoing sailing ship.
Overpopulation of the limited farmland, which
could not supply all their food needs, and the
appeal of foreign trade led to the Norwegian
Viking expeditions westward. The term Viking is
thought to come from the Old Norse word *vik*,
meaning creek. Thus a Viking was one who lived
near a creek.

Although the Vikings are mostly known for
pillaging Britain and Ireland, many of them settled
there, influencing the language and culture of
their new homes. They also colonized Iceland,
Greenland, and the Faroe Islands. And around
1000 CE the mariner and adventurer Leif Eriksson
was striking even further west to North America
to found the colony he called Vinland, probably
Newfoundland.

The benefits of the Viking raids were felt
throughout Norway, not only in the spoils
of war, but in new skills and
knowledge acquired overseas.
Farmland was increased by
means of slaves brought in
to work on land clearance.

The Arrival of Christianity
In 1015 Olav Haraldsson, a Viking chieftain, set
sail for Norway from England, where he had
established a power base. With one hundred men

he successfully conquered and united his homeland, which had been divided by the inheritance battles of the sons and grandsons of Harald. During a reign of twelve peaceful years, he founded Norway's first national government. Justice was administered in each region by the Ting (literally, the "Thing," the court), run on broadly democratic lines. While in England he had been converted to Christianity and now imposed this new faith on his heathen subjects, although paganism was still in evidence for several centuries.

Following a successful Danish invasion, King Olav was forced to flee in 1028. His return two years later with insufficient forces to regain his

kingdom ended in defeat and death. During the following decade Norwegians became increasingly resentful of their new Danish king and in retrospect the memory of Olav grew more and more heroic. Popular tales of miracles wrought by his body were rapidly seized upon by the Norwegian Church. Olav was canonized and his remains were buried at Nidaros (Trondheim), where stories of miracles abounded and helped to increase the Christian flock.

Medieval Times—Power Gained and Lost

With the return of a Norwegian king (Magnus)
and treaties with Denmark, years of peace and
economic prosperity saw out the eleventh century.
For the next two hundred years, despite periods of
civil war, Norway continued to consolidate its
position as an independent
power. King Håkon VI
established royal authority over
the nobility and the Church,
and made the monarchy
hereditary. Greenland and
Iceland were brought under Norwegian rule and
its hold was strengthened on the Shetland and
Faroe Islands.

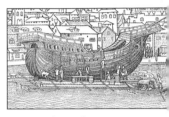

Throughout this time law and order were
maintained and trade flourished, largely through
the endeavors of the Hanseatic League, a trading
association of European and Baltic cities. The
most prominent Norwegian town to belong to
this league was Bergen. As the merchants grew in
power, controlling imports and inland trade, the
monarchy grew more and more dependent on
taxes levied on the Hanseatic League traders.

In 1349 the Black Death arrived in Norway,
spreading rapidly along the coast, through the
fjords and valleys, and wiping out two-thirds of
the population. Huge numbers of farms were left
unpopulated or abandoned. This resulted not

only in years of famine, but also in the decimation of the nobility who relied on their rent. Local government collapsed and, on the death of King Håkon VI in 1380, the struggles for the throne, which had been ongoing through these medieval years, saw the end of Norway as an independent power for the next five hundred years.

Uneasy Unions

On the death of Håkon VI, Norway came under the control of his son Olav in union with the powerful and clever Danish Princess Margrethe. On Olav's death she masterminded a union of Norway, Denmark, and Sweden,  convincing the nobles of all three nations to install her as regent and accept her young nephew Erik as king. The Kalmar Union was so named following the coronation of Erik in Kalmar in 1397.

After Margrethe's death in 1412 Denmark was the center of power. Erik's incompetence led to Sweden leaving the union and to the impoverishment of Norway as it was taxed to pay for his brutal wars. In 1450 a Danish noble, Count Christian of Oldenburg, was crowned king of Norway and Denmark. As Danish became the official language, leading positions in state and Church were held by Danes, and Norway lost any sway in Scandinavian affairs.

Union with Denmark

By 1536 Norway was little more than a Danish
dependency, valued only for its iron ore, fish, and
timber. These were a constant source of conflict
between Sweden and Denmark and the country
suffered devastation as they vied for its spoils.

A century of bureaucracy and monopoly
imposed by Denmark ended in the 1760s when
trade barriers with foreign countries were
abolished. The economy boomed and overseas
trade, especially with England, prospered in the
years leading up to the Napoleonic Wars.
Norway's merchants profited from the increased
demand for naval supplies. Denmark and Norway
remained neutral in this conflict, but when
Napoleon instituted a trade blockade against
Britain and drew Denmark in, Britain retaliated
by bombarding Copenhagen. Denmark declared
war on England and Sweden in 1807, bringing
great hardship to Norway through loss of trade.

When Napoleon was defeated Norway was
ceded to Sweden as part of the 1814 Kiel Peace
Agreement and a four-century union was
dissolved. It retained its own parliament but the
cabinet was appointed by the King of Sweden.

Union with Sweden

Having shaken off dependency on the Danes, the
Norwegians were unhappy to find themselves

subservient to the Swedes. The popular desire now was for independence. On May 17, 1814, a constitution, still in effect today, was unveiled, declaring Norway to be a "free, independent, and indivisible realm."

Though it recognized this constitution and the Norwegian parliament, Sweden retained a veto over Norway's actions, and all foreign affairs remained in Swedish hands. However, domestic independence prospered and Norway enjoyed a period of economic growth and reform. The sense of national confidence and identity grew and art, literature, and music flourished.

Despite these encouraging signs, this was a time of mass exodus. The population had doubled, and the lack of sufficient farmland and rural poverty, coupled with tales of overseas opportunity, led to almost half the people emigrating, mainly to North America, during the nineteenth century.

Independence
By the end of the century, demands for independence were louder than ever. In August 1905 Norway voted overwhelmingly to dissolve the union with Sweden and to become an independent

monarchy. A Danish prince, Karl, was elected to the throne as King Håkon VII.

The introduction of hydroelectric power led to the harnessing of Norway's natural resources. Under a Liberal government industry developed and wealth grew, helping to fund social reform. A powerful trade union movement emerged and was represented by the Labor Party. By 1913 suffrage had been granted to all men and women.

The War Years—Attempted Neutrality
Despite declaring itself neutral at the outbreak of the First World World, Norway found itself negatively impacted by action around its coast. Dependent as it was on shipping, trade was adversely affected by blockades and strict trade embargoes imposed by the Western Allies. The bitter war at sea was no respecter of neutral shipping and Norway had lost half its merchant fleet by the end of the war.

The economic depression that swept the Western world in the 1920s and '30s led to the rise in power of the Labor Party, which has been a powerful force in Norwegian politics ever since.

Norway joined the League of Nations in 1920 and followed a policy of peace and disarmament. On the outbreak of the Second World War, Norway once again declared itself neutral and was taken by surprise in early 1940 when it awoke to

German invasion. King Håkon
VII escaped to London, from
where he worked with the
Norwegian exile movement.

The politician Vidkun
Quisling—whose name has
become synonymous with
traitor—was declared "Minister
President" by the Nazis, but Norwegian civil and
military resistance grew in strength as the
occupation continued and many important
sabotage operations took place. Once again
Norway's terrain played an important role, making
it difficult for the Nazis to control a land divided by
mountain and fjord. On the German surrender,
King Håkon returned to great celebrations.

The Postwar Years
The retreating Germans burned their way out of
Norway, leaving much destruction in the north.
Most of the merchant fleet had been overseas at
the time of the country's invasion and had then
joined the Allied forces. Heavy losses had halved
the shipping stock and industry had all but
stopped production.

The great spirit of unity in a still young
country regaining its independence meant that
recovery was rapid. With economic growth came
further social reform and the introduction of the

welfare state. The wealth-generating industries of hydroelectricity, mining, and steel production were state owned, providing the nation with the resources to eradicate poverty and to create an increasingly egalitarian country. From 1945 to 1965 Labor governments introduced economic planning and permanent price controls.

Norway Today

Today Norway is one of the wealthiest countries in the world with a high standard of living for all. National pride and identity are very important to Norwegians. Although it is a modern society, which embraces changes in technology quickly, it still values the traditional way of life and respects the place of nature. This can be seen in the importance placed on family, the support for small communities, and the rural life which many urban and suburban Norwegians return to in their country cabins.

Rarely in the forefront of world events and willing to stand alone on occasion, Norway is nevertheless a team player, taking a quietly active role in the promotion of peace. Although a halt was put on immigration in 1975, the great influx of migrants in the 1960s and more recently the acceptance of large numbers of both specialist workers and asylum seekers have led to Norway gradually becoming a more diverse and multicultural society—in the larger towns at least.

You could say that Norway has it all—wealth and beauty—and yet it is still largely undiscovered by the rest of the world. If the truth were told, that is probably the way the Norwegians prefer it.

NORWAY'S TOWNS

It is perhaps an indication of Norway's size, or its inherent modesty, that Norwegian has no word for city. Even Oslo, the nation's capital, is a *stor by*, a big town. With a population of 510,000 and a metropolitan area of 900,000 it is certainly

Norway's largest town. Situated in the southwest of the country at the head of the Oslofjord, it is an attractive city with an interesting waterfront and is the home of

both monarch and government. As the gateway to Norway, it is also an important center for international shipping.

Bergen, once a major trading center and the former west coast capital of Norway, is now its second town. Its population of 200,000 have made their homes around the scenic harbor and amongst the seven hills on which the town is built. Although beautiful, its topography means that it is often shrouded in cloud and it can be quite difficult to visit Bergen when it is not raining! Known as the "Capital of the Fjords," and proud of its cosmopolitan air and academic and cultural history, Bergen is a popular stopping off place for cruise liners and tourist ships.

Although the medieval town of Trondheim is Norway's third-largest town, the pace of life is slow and leisurely. Celebrating its thousandth anniversary in 1997, Trondheim was home to the ancient Norse parliament and its most famous landmark today is the beautiful cathedral, Nidaros Domkirke, Scandinavia's largest surviving medieval structure. Situated in mid-Norway, just west of the busy rail junction of Hell (yes, really!), Trondheim is a center of excellence for engineering and technical training.

Norway's oil capital, Stavanger, on the southwestern coast, is a thriving industrial center. Its wealth has always come from the sea—first through shipbuilding, then fish canning, and now from its offshore oil wells. Of its 100,000 plus population, 10 percent are foreigners. With a NATO base and many overseas oil companies situated here, English is an easy second language.

Rather bizarrely dubbed the "Paris of the North," and situated far north of the Arctic Circle, Tromsø is the world's most northern university and cathedral town. With a population of 60,000, it is easily the largest center in northern Norway.

GOVERNMENT AND POLITICS

Norway has a constitutional monarchy. The 165 members of the *Storting* (Parliament) are elected by proportional representation to serve fixed four-year terms. The decisions of the government are formalized by the king and then implemented by the ministries. General suffrage for men was introduced in 1898 and for women in 1913. Election turnout is high, usually around 80 percent of the population ages eighteen and over.

Political Parties

Over twenty political parties, covering a broad spectrum—left/right, moral/religious, geographical, and environmental—are registered in Norway. In practice, only a small number are represented in the *Storting*. As we have seen, from before the Second World War until the 1960s the Norske Arbedierpartiet (Labor Party) dominated Norwegian politics. As the nation's wealth grew and was invested in the country's infrastructure and distributed to its population, there was a move toward the center and right in Norwegian politics. This is thought to be the result, not only of the country's oil wealth, but also of the problems associated with increased immigration.

Although there have been Labor governments since then, there has been a tendency toward more coalition governments, with no single party holding a majority. Since 1997 center-right coalitions have been in place under Prime Minister Kjell Magne Bondevik of the Christian Democrats. His party, together with the Center Party, has been part of all nonsocialist governments since 1963.

NORWEGIAN OIL

With the discovery of oil offshore in the North Sea and Norwegian Sea in the late 1960s, Norway entered the oil age. By 1975 the nation had become a net exporter of oil and gas and today only Russia and Saudi Arabia export more oil than Norway. As a natural offshoot, the engineering industry has also expanded. Today 64,000 Norwegians work in the oil sector.

Perhaps it is the way that Norway has used the income from this highly lucrative industry that distinguishes it. Like any sensible family with a windfall, they have spent some and saved some. Revenue was first plowed into the country's declining industries and used to improve the transportation, education, and health systems. As a result, all Norwegians benefited and the country's standard of living grew markedly. But, although gas supplies are likely to last beyond the oil, many

worry about the day when reserves finally dry up.
As protection against this time, Norway has been
saving in a Government Petroleum Fund,
currently valued at tens of billions of dollars.

NORWAY'S PLACE IN THE REGION
Nordic Neighbors

The Nordic countries share a common culture as well
as similarities of language and character. Their shared
history has not always been without conflict and
rivalry, but overall more similarities than differences
remain. The Nordic Council was formed in 1952
when Scandinavian neighbors Denmark, Sweden,
Norway, and Finland formalized their cooperative
relationship with Iceland, Greenland, and the Faroe
Islands to "achieve more together than the individual
countries are capable of achieving on their own." Not
only do member states agree upon pan-Nordic action
plans on issues such as environmental protection, but
citizens may work and study in each other's countries
as well as make use of health services with little
interference from bureaucracy.

The European Union

Unlike its Scandinavian neighbors, Norway has
twice rejected the opportunity to join the European
Union. It might seem curious that such a small
country, with its proximity to the important

markets of Western Europe, should vote against E.U. membership. But this it did, albeit narrowly, in referenda in 1972 and 1994. In all likelihood this decision came more from the heart than the bank balance. Having taken so long to achieve the dream of independence, Norway was not easily going to surrender to the bureaucrats of Brussels. However, since 1994 Norway has been a signatory of the European Economic Agreement, a free trade agreement that allows citizens to seek work in member states.

So far, Norway's rejection of the E.U. does not seem to have hindered its success. Norway is still in its early years and enjoying its independence. It is also a country that knows its own mind, but that does not mean it follows an isolationist policy. Norway was one of the founding members of the United Nations in 1945 and the first UN Secretary-General, Tryggve Lie, was a Norwegian. Norway also joined NATO in 1949.

The Schengen Agreement
The Schengen Agreement aims gradually to abolish checks at common borders. Citizens of countries implementing the agreement can cross the internal borders of each other's countries without check. Norway signed the agreement in 2001, joining fourteen other countries including France, Germany, Spain, and the Scandinavian nations.

chapter two

VALUES & ATTITUDES

A history of survival in a difficult, isolated landscape and often harsh climate has forged a people that are hardworking, ruggedly self-sufficient, and reserved. From Viking times local parliaments displayed the basic democratic principles that have engendered the spirit of equality and fairness that pervades Norway today. Union with neighboring nations has fostered a spirit of consensus rather than confrontation. The long struggle for independence has brought about an idealistic nationalism. A coastline of 13,700 miles (21,900 km) has inspired a love of the sea and exploration, while the majestic landscape has commanded a respect for nature. In this way the national values and attitudes of Norway have been shaped.

COOPERATION

With the strong emphasis placed on teamwork from the earliest age, Norwegians generally have no problem cooperating to produce a solution to a problem. This spirit of cooperation is best demonstrated in the popular Norwegian practice of *dugnad.*

The *dugnad* is a collective effort, a work-sharing activity where people contribute as volunteers. For example, a school may hold a *dugnad* to clean up the school grounds one Saturday. Parents and pupils will turn up and all play their part in smartening up the school. The local football club may hold a *dugnad* to paint the clubhouse. Members and their families will all help to get the job done. Environmental organizations also often hold *dugnads* to involve local people in conservation or cleanup projects.

In difficult terrain and climate, you never know when you may need to rely on the cooperation of others. If you run your car off the road into a snowdrift and start digging the vehicle out, it will not be long before someone stops and appears beside you with his shovel. In all likelihood few words will be exchanged, but your companion will help to get you back on the road.

FAIRNESS

In Norway it is seen as fair that every member of society should receive enough. Those with high earnings pay higher taxes to help compensate those who are less fortunate or less successful. The welfare state ensures that there is equal access to education, health care, and social security for all.

This fairness is highly visible. Records are also open to all. For example, for three weeks after the annual tax returns are confirmed as official, they are published on the Internet. Everyone may easily see their neighbor's salary and how much tax they pay.

EQUALITY
According to the United Nations Human Development Report, Norway is ranked as the world's leading nation in the field of gender equality. Women were granted the vote in 1913 and the first female prime minister, Gro Harlem Brundtland, took office in 1981. Currently head of the World Health Organization, Dr. Brundtland has said that many countries look to Norway for inspiration on how to promote sexual equality.

Although gender equality is broadly entrenched in Norwegian society, legislation has still been necessary to ensure that women are adequately represented in the decision-making process. Norway was the first country in the world to appoint a Gender Equality Ombudsman and for the last twenty years women have made up almost half of Norwegian governments and 60 percent of university graduates. The 1987 ruling, requiring that at least 40 percent of each gender be represented on public boards and committees, is now to be enforced in the private sector.

The law also protects the working rights of pregnant women and new mothers. Norway was a pioneer in paternity leave. On the birth of a child, parents are entitled to forty-eight weeks' leave, which may be shared between them. In practice, it is the woman who takes the leave and steps are in place to encourage fathers to take at least four weeks' paternity leave.

In terms of breaking into traditional male roles, you are more likely to see a woman driving a bus, working on road construction, and working as an engineer in the oil industry in Norway than elsewhere.

Despite massive leaps forward, with men playing a far greater role in the domestic sphere, women still retain the greater part of responsibility for the home and children. Many work part-time and juggle work, home, and a nurturer's duties. As a result, despite their education and training, their priorities may differ from those of their male colleagues and mean that they are not always in a position to gain sufficient experience to take on the most demanding business roles.

Compared with many other countries, Norway is doing well in the equality stakes. However, disparities still remain. Women generally earn 85 percent of the salary men earn. While this was impressive in the 1980s, there has been little change over the last twenty years and in the view of many women there is still work to be done.

PUNCTUALITY

Punctuality is important to Norwegians, who like to arrive on time. This is part of their culture of fairness and respect for all. Everyone's time is of equal value so it is thoughtless to arrive too early or too late.

Do not ever make the mistake of thinking a Norwegian train, bus, or ferry will be running late. In most cases they leave exactly on time.

PATIENCE

A society that accepts that everyone's needs are equal also accepts that one must be patient and wait one's turn. Equality and fairness mean that no one pushes themselves forward or believes their business is more urgent.

In many banks, post offices, and other places where it is necessary to wait in line an automated queuing system has been introduced. On entry to the premises you take a *nummerlapp* (numbered ticket) and wait for your number to come up on the electronic display screen.

While the automated queuing system ensures that customers will be attended to in a fair order, it does not guarantee they will be attended to quickly. Long lines do not faze those who service them. Norwegians work at their own speed. Such places are excellent for picking out foreigners. They are the red-faced ones with steam coming out of their ears, seething under their breath at the three or four cashiers chatting in the corner while only two tellers are serving! Norwegians, seemingly oblivious, wait on patiently, no matter how long it takes.

NATURAL RESERVE

While Norway is a friendly, welcoming country, its people are far from effusive. Centuries of living in small, isolated communities have made them reserved by nature. Tending to socialize with family and friends with whom they have grown up, Norwegians are not naturally outgoing toward newcomers, and it is quite common to exchange no more than a very cursory nod with your neighbor for many years.

There is no real shortcut to breaking down this reserve; it just takes time. Questions about family and personal life that an American or Briton would view as showing polite interest could be construed as intrusive by Norwegians.

This natural reserve, coupled with a sense of earnestness, can make Norwegians appear very serious. However, when the occasion is right their dry sense of humor is highly visible, and they certainly know how to party!

CRADLE TO GRAVE SECURITY

Norway is a welfare state. Through membership of the Norwegian National Insurance Scheme, all its citizens (and those working in Norway) are entitled to a range of pensions and benefits that span the stages of life. Pensions are provided, for example, for the aged, disabled, widowed, and orphaned. Benefits in connection with pregnancy, birth, childhood, illness, unemployment, accidents, and funerals are also payable. Norway is unusual in paying parents to stay at home with their children. Those who do not send their child to a kindergarten are entitled to a benefit of NKr 3,600 (approximately U.S. $550, £300) per month under the "Cash for Care" scheme.

WEALTH AND GENEROSITY

The world of the twenty-first century is one in which energy equals wealth. With its natural resources of oil and hydroelectric power, Norway is one of the richest countries.

Norway has invested its wealth to benefit its citizens, but it is also generous to the world's poor and disadvantaged. The nation spends more money per capita on foreign aid than any other country in the world. Following the devastation of the Asian tsunami of December 2004, Norway's donation to the relief effort was the single-largest per capita pledge of any nation.

Situated in a fairly wealthy area of the world, Norwegians nevertheless help their "neighbors in need." Local churches and schools are the focal point for forging links with impoverished areas of Russia. Clothes, toiletries, toys, and food items are collected and regular deliveries are made to the linked communities.

ROYALTY

When Norway's union with Sweden was peacefully dissolved in 1905, the Norwegian people's desire was for their new nation to be a monarchy rather than a republic. A Danish prince was elected to the throne as King Håkon VII. He and his English wife, Queen Maud (youngest daughter of Edward VII), dedicated themselves to embracing and representing Norwegian culture. Known as the "People's King," Håkon dispensed with much of the pomp of royalty. When Germany invaded Norway in 1940, he  resolutely resisted its demands. After refusing to hand over authority to Quisling, he moved to London, where he became a focal point for Norway's resistance forces. On the German surrender, Håkon returned to a rousing welcome that ensured the popularity of the monarchy.

The constitutional monarchy has little real power, but acts as a symbol of unity. Today's Norwegian royal family, headed by King Harald V and Queen Sonja, conducts its affairs with the minimum of protocol and ceremony. Their two children grew up as far as possible like other children, attending local schools. Princess Martha Louise trained as a physical therapist and both she and her brother, Crown Prince Håkon, are active in the sports world.

However, the current cult of celebrity means that the lives of the two young royals feature prominently in newspapers and magazines. This reached its peak in 2000 when a furor arose over Crown Prince Håkon's engagement to an unmarried mother. The nation weathered the storm and the couple married the following year. Norwegians seem to have accepted Princess Mette-Marit as their future queen, particularly since the birth of little Princess Ingrid Alexandra in 2004.

GOD'S OWN COUNTRY

The UN Human Development Index, which measures the standard of living in nations around the world according to factors such as life expectancy, literacy, education, health, wealth, and equality, frequently places Norway at the top of the list. This only confirms what Norwegians already know. They live in a highly civilized society that strives for equality for all, where poverty is almost nonexistent and crime rates are low. In addition they have arguably the most beautiful scenery in Europe. Who would not wish to be born a Norwegian?

NATURE

The great outdoors plays a large part in Norwegian life and there is certainly plenty of it to enjoy—from forests and mountains to lakes and fjords. Norwegians seem to have instinctive love and respect for nature and are knowledgeable about the folklore that surrounds it.

The need to take advantage of the clean, fresh air and *å få fred og ro* (to find peace and calm) is recognized and valued in Norwegian society. Miles and miles of marked hiking trails (which in a straight line could actually extend from Oslo to Tokyo) are to be found throughout the country. Boating and fishing are popular pursuits on the many lakes and fjords.

Around one-third of Norwegians own a second home or *hytte* in the mountains or beside the sea where they spend weekends and holidays getting back to nature.

Enjoying nature is an all-year round experience. In the winter *å gå på tur* (to go for a walk) is replaced by *å gå på ski* (to go cross-country skiing). And what of the Norwegian climate, which can often make a day indoors seem attractive to foreigners? Norwegians will simply assure you that there is no such thing as bad weather, merely the wrong clothes.

EVERYMAN'S RIGHT

While Norwegians have a respect for private property, they also believe that nature is for all and should be enjoyed as freely as possible by as many as possible. An unofficial law, known as the right of passage, permits public right of access to uncultivated land anywhere, providing no damage or harm is caused. So you may walk, picnic, or set up a tent on any uncultivated land. You may also pick berries and mushrooms. In the winter you may cross by foot or ski cultivated land that is frozen or covered in snow.

Those taking advantage of this right of access are required to do so with a sense of respect for landowners, other country users, and the natural environment.

NORWEGIAN QUALITY

Norwegians are very proud of home-produced goods and services and have great faith in the quality of these. However, in a land of high wages and high taxes, home-produced goods and services tend to be expensive. When queried on this, Norwegians will simply tell you, with only a hint of smugness, that you are paying for "Norwegian quality."

Per og Kari

This imaginary pair, representing Mr. and Mrs. Norway, the average couple with two children, is often referred to in advertisements and newspaper and television reports. Market researchers and pollsters discover where Per and Kari go on vacation, what they buy, what car they drive, their opinion on certain issues, and so on. Representing "middle Norway," Per og Kari are sometimes the butt of metropolitan Oslo humor!

WORK TO LIVE, NOT LIVE TO WORK

For Norwegians, maintaining a work–life balance is very important. They are hardworking, and production rates are high. The working week averages 37.5 to 40 hours and the working day in most companies runs from 8:00 a.m. to 4:00 p.m. However, what often surprises visitors from more work-driven cultures is the Norwegian attitude to work and business.

Though they take their work seriously, leisure is also highly valued. Overtime is controlled and viewed with suspicion. While an American, for example, may be shocked to see an office emptying on the stroke of 4:00 p.m., Norwegians will wonder why he needs to work late into the evening. Perhaps he is incompetent or slow.

High rates of taxation also lessen the appeal of overtime, as does the arrival of summer. Norwegians are entitled to three consecutive weeks of summer vacation and many offices and businesses, banks, and post offices have shorter hours in the summer, closing early in June–August. The Norwegian summer is too short and too glorious to be spent sitting in an office.

CONSENSUS AND NONCONFRONTATION

As part of their natural reserve, Norwegians back away from high emotion and confrontation.

Causing a scene, becoming angry, or making your point by shouting and gesticulating would make you look foolish and uncontrolled in the eyes of Norwegians. They would be shocked and very uncomfortable at such conduct and would certainly lose respect for someone behaving in such a manner.

Nonconfrontation in Action

Lack of confrontation was taken to extremes after a minor road accident. A small van containing two young men ran into the back of a family car that had stopped at a pedestrian crossing. Drivers and passengers got calmly out of their vehicles, inspected the damage, exchanged insurance details, and immediately got on their mobile phones. There were no expletives, no reprimands, only the bare minimum of communication. Then both parties got back into their cars and awaited the arrival of the roadside assistance.

ATTITUDES TO FOREIGNERS

Although polite and helpful, Norwegians are not overly enthusiastic about foreigners. While not necessarily regarding themselves as superior to other Europeans in general, they certainly would not see themselves as inferior to any race.

In 1975 a ban was imposed on immigration and, until Norway's membership in the European Economic Agreement in 1994, obtaining a work permit was very difficult for those not offering the specialist skills needed for the oil industry. Today, with an aging (and long-living) population and a shortage of specialist skills, Norway is actively recruiting workers to fill the shortfall, with large numbers coming from Russia. In addition, Norway takes its annual quota of refugees.

It is perhaps natural then that a nation with a great sense of pride in the society it has created and respect for its own traditions and values should be a little wary of the change it worries may result from immigration from very different cultures. Problems with Mafia-style crime, especially among Vietnamese, Asian, and Bosnian groups, have unsettled many and an increase in violent crime in the border regions of the north is blamed on Russian neighbors. In fact, it is common in conversation among Norwegians to hear the ills of their modern society blamed on immigrants. Although Norway remains a tolerant country where human rights and civil liberties are well respected, xenophobic attitudes are becoming more acceptable. Incidents of discrimination against ethnic minorities have been reported, and it is clear that racism is on the increase.

Norwegians, however, will not admit to this.

Tourists and foreign workers on temporary contracts are welcome, but on the whole most Norwegians would prefer to keep Norway for the Norwegians.

Centuries of union with, or subservience to, its nearest Scandinavian neighbors have left a love–hate relationship. Gross caricatures, exploited in jokes and cartoons, can be found: the Finn has rather too much liking for his liquor, the Swede is not well-endowed with brains, the Dane is happy-go-lucky but his thick accent is caused by speaking "with a potato in his mouth." However, the Nordic countries stand together on so many issues and their bonds are so strong, that a little sibling antagonism is understandable.

chapter three

CUSTOMS &
TRADITIONS

As a relatively young country, at least in terms of its present constitution, Norway has needed to establish its identity over the last century. One of the ways it has done this is through the fostering of customs and traditions. While many of these are religious in origin and therefore not specifically Norwegian, it is the way in which they are celebrated that provides the national flavor.

In this country where sun and light are so important, the majority of holidays and celebration days take place in spring and summer. May, which is possibly the most beautiful month in Norway, has more than its fair share of public holidays. No wonder it is often said that no one does any work in May!

THE NORWEGIAN YEAR
Norway has ten legal holidays per year, most of them religion based. If a national holiday, such as Christmas Day, falls on a weekend there is no day

off in lieu as in some other countries. (In the
tables, the legal holidays appear in bold type.)

DATE	NORWEGIAN HOLIDAY	ENGLISH NAME
January 1	***Nyttårsdag***	**New Year's Day**
Feb./March	*Søndag før Faste (Fastelavnssøndag)*	Sunday before Lent
March/April	***Skjærtorsdag***	**Maundy/ Holy Thursday**
March/April	***Langfredag***	**Good Friday**
March/April	*Påskedag*	Easter Day
March/April	***2. Påskedag***	**Easter Monday**
May 1	***Offentlig høytidsdag***	**Labor Day**
May 8	*Frigjøringsdag 1945*	Liberation Day 1945
May	***Kristihimmelfartsdag***	**Ascension Day**
May 17	***Grunnlovsdag***	**Constitution Day (Norway's National Day)**
May/June	*Pinsedag*	Pentecost/Whit Sunday
May/June	***2. Pinsedag***	**Pentecost/Whit Monday**
June 23	*Sankthans*	Midsummer's Eve
End October	*Bots- og bededag*	Day of Penance and Prayer
October/Nov.	*Allehelgensdag*	All Saints' Day
November	*1. Søndag i Advent*	First Sunday in Advent
December 13	*Santa Lucia*	Saint Lucy
December 24	*Julaften*	Christmas Eve
December 25	***Juledag***	**Christmas Day**
December 26	***2. Juledag***	**Boxing Day**

FLAG FLYING DAYS

Norwegians are fiercely patriotic. Not only do all
official buildings fly the Norwegian flag on notable
dates, but many homes have a flagpole in the
garden. Strict rules govern the times at which the

DATE	NORWEGIAN FLAG DAY	ENGLISH NAME
January 1	*Nyttårsdag*	**New Year's Day**
January 21	*Prinsesse Ingrid Alexandras fødselsdag*	*Princess Ingrid Alexandra's birthday*
February 6	*Samefolketsdag*	*Sami* People's Day
February 21	*Kong Harald Vs fødselsdag*	*King Harald V's* birthday
March/April	*Påskedag*	Easter Day
May 1	*Offentlig høytidsdag*	**Labor Day**
May 8	*Frigjøringsdag 1945*	Liberation Day 1945
May 17	*Grunnlovsdag*	**Constitution Day (Norway's National Day)**
May/June	*Pinsedag*	Pentecost/Whit Sunday
June 7	*Unionsoppløsningen 1905*	Dissolution of the Union 1905
July 4	*Dronning Sonjas fødselsdag*	Queen Sonja's birthday
July 20	*Kronprins Håkons fødselsdag*	Crown Prince Håkon's birthday
July 29	*Olsokdag*	St Olav's Day
August 19	*Kronprinsesse Mette-Marits fødselsdag*	Crown Princess Mette-Marit's birthday
December 25	*Juledag*	**Christmas Day**

flags should be raised and lowered. In addition to the official flag flying days listed below, Norwegians are permitted to fly the flag for special family occasions. A local or national tragedy will also be marked by the flying of flags at half-mast.

RELIGIOUS FESTIVALS
Advent

Light plays an important role in the dark month of Advent. On the fourth Sunday before Christmas the first of the four candles in the Advent crown is lit. This not only represents the religious symbolism of Christ, the light of the world, but also continues the old tradition in Norwegian homes of placing a lighted candle at the window to guide travelers through the long northern winter.

Today, throughout Advent, lights in the form of electric candle-bridges or stars shine in the windows of almost every home. In the gardens, lights are placed on fir trees, and towns are festooned with lanterns. A welcoming candle (often in the snow) greets you at the door of any gathering, where you will be offered warm *gløgg* (mulled wine) and *pepperkaker* (heart-shaped ginger biscuits).

Santa Lucia

On December 13 primary schoolchildren celebrate the feast of Santa Lucia, a young girl

from Roman times who suffered for her faith.
Children, dressed in white with silver tinsel in
their hair, carry candles to represent faith and
light in the darkness of winter. Often parents and
guests are invited to the school to hear the
children sing special songs.

Christmas (*Jul*)

Unlike more commercialized societies where
Christmas arrives in the shops in
September, Norway's Christmas does not
begin until December. Then, boats filled
with trees anchor in coastal towns and the
quaysides are full of families choosing
trees. Inland, many buy theirs from tree
farms. The tree is taken home and
decorated with white lights, wooden
ornaments, and baked gingerbread hearts
trimmed with white icing and red ribbon.
A wreath is placed on the door and a sheaf of
corn hung up outside for the birds. Families
gather in the late afternoon of December 24 for
Christmas dinner. Depending on the area of
Norway this could be *pinnekjøtt* (salted dried
lamb steamed over birch), *ribbe* (roast belly pork),
lutefisk (dried cod preserved in caustic soda), or
reindeer. A creamy rice pudding (*rømmegrøt*) and
little cookies complete the meal. Then presents are
exchanged and the children may find that the

julenisse (Christmas elf) has left some surprises. December 25 provides another opportunity for families to get together in celebration while December 26 is a day of relaxation.

Like many of their Scandinavian neighbors, Norwegians are increasingly fond of escaping the cold and darkness of winter for sunnier climes at this time of year.

Easter (*Påske*)

During Lent birch twigs are brought indoors and decorated with feathers. The buds, breaking into green shoots, symbolize the approach of spring. As well as being a religious celebration, Easter is a popular five-day holiday in Norway. Towns are often deserted as people head for their cabins in the mountains for the last skiing of the year. Those staying at home may begin spring-cleaning, outdoor renovation, or preparing their boats for a return to the water.

Ascension Day (*Kristihimmelfartsdag*)

Falling on the Thursday five and a half weeks after Easter, this public holiday is usually taken as a long weekend to enjoy the spring weather.

Whitsun (*Pinsedag*)

Pentecost/Whit Sunday falls ten days after Ascension Day. The following day, Whit

Monday, is another public holiday, which allows
Norwegians to enjoy a long weekend.

NONRELIGIOUS CELEBRATIONS
New Year's Eve (*Nyttårsaften*)
The New Year is a time to celebrate with
fireworks. Larger towns may put on public
displays, but most people get together with
friends and families for fireworks outside their
homes. Unlike many countries, there is no

waiting for the chimes of midnight.
Throughout the evening fireworks are
lit and from about 11:30 p.m. there is
a gloriously chaotic cacophony of
noise and color as everyone in the
neighborhood joins in the display!

Labor Day (*Offentlig høytidsdag*)
May 1 is celebrated, as throughout much of
Europe, as Labor Day. This is when workers are
honored by parades of trade unions accompanied
by bands and banners. These are followed by
speeches made by political and workers' leaders at
public gatherings.

Russ—Crazy High School Leavers
At the age of eighteen or nineteen Norwegian
students graduate from high school. In the month

leading up to their final exams, which will soon be followed by the responsibilities of entering university or the working world, they celebrate the end of their compulsory school years by becoming *russ* and engaging in crazy *russefeiring* (*russ* activities).

The term *russ* originates from Latin, *Cornua Depositurus*, about to put aside one's horns. Dating back to the 1700s, when there were no universities in Norway, Norwegians wishing to study at a higher level had to attend the University of Copenhagen along with Danish students. In order to be enrolled at the university, students were required to take an examination. On completion of this, horns were placed on their foreheads and they were mocked by senior students. In a ceremony announcing the results of the exam, students were called to the examiner. If they had passed, their horns were removed as a sign

of wisdom and "subjugation of the wild animal within." They had now earned the right to call themselves students.

The *russ* are instantly recognizable in April and May. They wear overalls, baggy trousers, and a beret-style cap with a long string hanging from it. This uniform is color coded according to the subjects the student has studied, such as red for general studies, or blue for economics. Knots and objects attached to the beret string are earned by doing something silly or funny (and quite possibly illegal). An essential accessory is the *russ* calling card, which bears the individual's photograph, name, and nickname and a pithy summary of the *russ*'s opinions on some subject. These cards are handed out to all and sundry. Children collect and trade *russ* cards.

For these few weeks this wild and noisy behavior is indulged. Their partying culminates in the *russeparade* of May 17 (Norway's National Day), when the *russ* parade through town, shouting slogans, blowing whistles, singing, and throwing water. Soon the final examinations start, and life returns to normal.

National Day (*Grunnlovsdag*)

Norway's national day, May 17, is the anniversary of the day in 1814 that the Norwegian constitution was laid down. If you are fortunate enough to be in Norway on May 17 (*syttende mai*), then you will witness Norway's colorful and amiable demonstration of its national pride.

In every town and village the day begins with a parade of all the schoolchildren, accompanied by their teachers and school bands. All along the route, lined by townsfolk, they sing traditional songs and wave flags.

Everyone is smartly dressed and *bunad* (Norway's traditional costume) is out in force. These folk costumes vary in color and design from region to region but women usually wear an embroidered woolen skirt  and waistcoat, perhaps with a bonnet, shawl, or white apron. Silver jewelry in the form of belts, buckles, and decorations is added throughout the wearer's life. Men wear a shirt, fitted black jacket, knee-length trousers, and stockings.

After the schoolchildren the *russ* parade in their colorful uniforms, and then the ordinary people, members of churches, football teams, clubs, and bands take to the streets. Everyone is represented and everywhere the Norwegian flag flies.

After the parade the schools are the focus for refreshments and entertainment for the children. Families assemble and enjoy a good meal together. The Norwegians have much to be proud of and this day of national celebration is a joyful and unifying occasion.

Midsummer (*Sankthans*)

The height of summer is a time for celebration. The longest day of the year, when the sun barely sets in the south and has not set for weeks in the far north, thrives on the magical mystery of pagan times. Traditionally trees talk, trolls run amok, and elves play tricks on mortals.

Today neighborhoods get together to celebrate

with huge bonfires. *Pølser* (sausages) are grilled, children take part in communal games and races, folk music is played, and adults have a drink or two. Many go out in boats to enjoy the spectacle of bonfires lighting up the coastline.

RELIGION

Norway's official Protestant State Church is Evangelical Lutheran and has the monarch as its head. Although there is no church and state separation, religious freedom is guaranteed to all. The Church is allocated funding from general taxes, based on its list of affiliated members. Other faith groups may also claim "church tax" for their registered members.

While roughly 90 percent of Norwegians

belong to the Church of Norway, only 10 percent attend church services or meetings with any regularity. Although most claim that religion is important to them (and the Church is still popular for baptisms, weddings, and funerals), today many express their spirituality through communion with nature. Men and women have equal rights to hold positions within the Church.

Other religious groups are small, forming about 5 percent of the population. For them the most problematic religious policy issue is the compulsory teaching of Christian catechism in all public schools.

FAMILY OCCASIONS
Baptism (*barnedåp*)
Most babies are baptized into the Church of Norway. Usually two sets of godparents are appointed who vow to safeguard the child's moral and spiritual growth. After the service a family celebration takes place with a lunch or small party, when gifts are presented to the baby.

Confirmation (*konfirmasjon*)
Confirmation is an important occasion and something of a rite of passage for 14–15 year olds. Through the weeks preceding the ceremony, often

held in May, they attend a course of classes preparing them for their vow to accept the principles of the Church of Norway.

The confirmation service takes place in the local church, and the families have big celebratory lunch parties. These are popular occasions to wear the *bunad,* especially for females. Photographs are taken and the confirmands are presented with gifts. Silver jewelry and ornaments for the *bunad* are popular with girls, but increasingly the confirmands receive money or expensive gifts.

Today there is some skepticism about the confirmation ritual. Many claim that most youngsters take part for purely mercenary reasons, wanting the special day, the party, and the gifts, but are unlikely to set foot inside the church often thereafter. Some atheists or agnostics even undergo a civil confirmation, so as not to miss out on the party and gifts!

Weddings

Around two-thirds of Norwegian weddings take place in church, with the remainder civil ceremonies. Interestingly, Norwegians are marrying later and increasing numbers are marrying foreigners and marrying overseas. However, the number of marriages is declining, with 50 percent of couples choosing to cohabit. Almost one-half of marriages will be dissolved before the silver wedding anniversary. Registered single-sex partnerships are also recognized in Norway.

Many brides today choose a white wedding dress instead of wearing the traditional national costume. A bridesmaid and best man witness the marriage and a celebratory meal and party follow.

Funerals

Funeral arrangements are published in the local newspaper, stating date, time, and place of the service. The National Insurance scheme awards a lump sum grant to cover funeral expenses. Today, anyone who so wishes may be cremated or buried with a nonreligious ceremony or, in fact, without any ceremony at all.

Most funeral services still take place in church, but nonreligious funerals are conducted in regular cemetery or crematorium chapels. In addition, an increase in the number of grave sites outside official cemeteries and the scattering of ashes in the mountains (only legally permitted since 1997) reflects the growing number of people embracing humanism.

chapter four

MAKING FRIENDS

Most Norwegians make their friends during their formative years, and it is around these relationships, as well as their family, that their social life revolves. Friends made at school or in childhood are likely to form the larger part of a Norwegian's social circle. Aside from large family gatherings, socializing is likely to happen in small groups where the conversation will be relaxed and interspersed with comfortable silences.

Norwegians are economical not only with words, but also with their friendship. Although polite and welcoming, they are naturally reserved and do not wear their hearts on their sleeves. Early conversation may be rather stilted and the foreign visitor may be tempted to fill the embarrassing pauses with personal comments or inquiries, which a Norwegian would find inappropriate at this stage in the acquaintance.

Norwegians who have traveled widely or who work in international companies, particularly in the oil and gas industries, are likely to be more forthcoming and accepting of the openness of others, but on the whole there is no substitute for taking time—plenty of time—to let friendship grow. Foreigners will need to earn the trust of their Norwegian acquaintances before they will be able to break through the barrier of reserve. It is realistic to think years, rather than months.

It Just Takes Time

One British woman, married to a Norwegian and living in Norway for over thirty years, tells of her surprise when she answered a knock at her door to find her next-door neighbor standing there. In the seventeen years they had been neighbors the woman had never offered more than a cursory nod to acknowledge her existence. Now, having locked herself out of the house, the neighbor had come to ask if she could use the telephone to summon help! For the next seventeen years the relationship moved forward. *God morgen* (good morning) now accompanied the nod.

WORK AND SOCIAL LIFE

Norwegians rarely mix business and pleasure. It is not common practice to go for a drink after work with colleagues. Team-building and socializing with colleagues are considered important in the Norwegian work culture, but they take place in a more formalized way. Many Norwegian companies have active sports and social clubs that organize social events. With the exception of the annual *julebord* (Christmas party), these functions are normally for employees only, without spouses or partners.

Typical events could be an evening trip to a local ski center, a summer barbecue, a boat trip, or a meal at a hotel. Also popular is the *blå tur*, or mystery tour, when employees board a chartered bus after work and are taken off to an unknown destination for a meal or activity.

While such occasions are to be enjoyed with colleagues, work is not a major place for making friends. Meeting and making friends with Norwegians is better attempted outside the formality of the working world.

Norwegian society is very much sport and leisure oriented, with all outdoor pursuits enjoying great popularity. Joining a gym, club, or organization that caters to such activities will bring you into contact with Norwegians in a less formal way.

GREETINGS

Norwegian greetings tend to be short and to the point. Although *g' morgen* (pronounced g' moren) may be used in the morning, usually *hei* or *hei hei* (pronounced somewhere between hi and hay) suffices for most greetings. Good-bye is *ha det bra*, literally have it good, often shortened to *ha det* (pronounced hadder).

There is no real informal use of please, but *takk* does the job for please and thank you. An expression you will hear everywhere, particularly in shops and restaurants, is *vær så god* (pronounced vair so goo). This is a bit of all-purpose politeness, which can mean "please," "you're welcome," or "thank you."

It is unusual to hear the use of Mr., Mrs., or Miss, unless a senior citizen is being addressed. Generally, first names are used. When meeting someone for the first time, whether at work or in a social  setting, it is common practice to shake hands and state your name and surname. Doctors, dentists, and lawyers will also introduce themselves in this way. Eye contact is very important in this situation.

HOSPITALITY

If you are fortunate enough to receive an invitation to a Norwegian home then you should not underestimate the honor bestowed upon you. While your invitation could be for the more informal *kaffe og kake* (coffee and cake), seasonal summer barbecue, or festive *gløgg og pepperkaker* (mulled wine and ginger cookies), it is more likely to be for dinner.

The perfect guest should arrive exactly on time with a small gift for the hostess. Flowers or a

 potted plant are always acceptable, as are chocolates. While wine would also be gratefully received, it is less commonly presented as a gift because of the laws regarding alcohol. Not only are there strict laws concerning the times at which alcohol may be sold, but wine and spirits are only available for sale at the state-controlled wine shop. As only one of these shops is permitted per *kommune* (administrative district) and as the tax on alcohol is high, guests may not always have the wherewithal to offer wine as a gift. Those who settle in Norway, but travel widely and have access to duty-free wine shops, may find themselves in a better position to make a gift of wine. It will be well received.

It is worth noting that the time stated on the invitation is the precise time at which you should arrive, as this is the time at which dinner will be served. While you may be offered one welcoming drink on arrival, it is not customary for Norwegians to stand around with predinner drinks for any length of time. You will very quickly be shown to your place at the table.

When your main course is served it will almost invariably be a meat dish. While fish dishes grow in popularity in other countries because of their health advantages, Norwegians still view fish, however sophisticatedly presented, as a throwback to earlier days when fish, fish, and fish was the staple diet of the country. They will be highly unlikely to select a fish dish in a restaurant or to serve it to guests.

Serving dishes will be passed around the table, and you should help yourself to only a small amount of each food offered. Don't take a large plateful, thinking that your hostess will be offended if no one takes much of her carefully prepared food. If the serving dish is emptied, she will be embarrassed, as the laws of hospitality state that there should be enough for everyone to have seconds.

Toasting is also an important aspect of the social dinner.

Norwegians incline their glasses toward one another and say *skål* (pronounced "skoal"), while making eye contact, first with their host and then with their fellow diners.

Larger functions and celebratory parties will be enhanced not only by toasts and speeches, but also by communal singing. Someone will have taken it upon themselves to customize the lyrics to well-known or traditional songs and distribute these to all the guests. The lyrics may be humorous or sentimental, but they will be relevant to those involved in the celebration, and everyone will join in with gusto.

After dinner, it is customary to retire to a comfortable sitting area for coffee and chocolates or *små kaker* (small cookies), after-dinner drinks and, of course, conversation.

GOOD MANNERS

Although Norway can seem a very casual and classless society, courtesy and a respect for age, tradition, and the environment are important.

Punctuality, which means arriving neither early nor late, but on time, shows respect for your host or business associate. A small gift demonstrates your appreciation for an invitation, as does your thanks by written note, telephone, or increasingly by e-mail message, afterwards. When you next meet someone with whom you have spent time, the phrase is *takk for sist* (literally "thanks for the last time"). Children will rise from the table offering *takk for maten* ("thanks for the food").

As we have seen, conversation can be stilted at first. Personal matters are never a suitable topic. Keeping conversation light and general is always the best policy. Complimenting Norway on its beautiful landscape is a winning icebreaker, as well as asking questions about local places of interest that you hope to visit. Sports are also a favorite subject, particularly among men. Norwegians are avid readers of newspapers and the discussion of politics (national and world) is certainly not taboo. Don't remark how expensive Norway is—they have heard it too often before.

GIFT GIVING
A small gift to your hostess in the form of flowers or chocolates is *de rigueur* when visiting a Norwegian home, but Norwegians are not extravagant gift givers. Friends will exchange birthday and Christmas presents, but unless it is a special birthday (one with a zero on the end, when a birthday cake may be served), it is not customary to give gifts to those you work with. However, an office collection may be made to buy a wedding present for a colleague.

DRESSING FOR THE OCCASION

You may be surprised, on your first visit to a
Norwegian bank or public office, to be served by
someone wearing jeans and a T-shirt. The dress
code in the working environment is casual: jeans,
T-shirts, sweaters. Managerial staff may wear
smarter clothes: casual trousers and open-necked
shirts. A business meeting might occasion the
addition of a sports jacket and possibly, at a very
important meeting, a tie. Never a suit!

Doctors, dentists, and medical staff wear their
loose-fitting work suits or casual clothes with
clogs and socks. In the winter, in particular, many
people change their outdoor footwear for indoor
shoes at work. These could be sandals with socks
or even carpet slippers.

It is well worth taking note of the Norwegian
saying "There is no such thing as bad weather,
only the wrong clothes." High quality wind-and-
waterproof clothing and footwear, made using the
latest technology, can make all the difference to
your Norwegian experience. There is much of
the great outdoors to enjoy and explore, but the
summer is short and waiting for a fine day
might take quite a while!

Norwegians dress according to the season,
and in winter hats are recommended. The
mother of any young child seen out hatless in
winter is likely to be advised by passing older

Norwegian women, "That child needs a hat."

Perhaps because the Norwegian dress code is generally so casual, people really seem to enjoy dressing up for special occasions like the annual *julebord* (Christmas party). Men will invariably wear a formal dark suit with shirt and tie, while a little black dress, sometimes with a few party sparkles, is favored by women.

LEARNING THE LANGUAGE

In Norway today English is taught from the first year of schooling and young Norwegians, motivated by the desire to learn the language of imported TV and movies, pop music, and the Internet, have considerable fluency in the language. In fact, it is usual to find that all but the most elderly people have a basic level of English and are happy to use it when confronted with visitors to their country.

Norwegians are realistic about their own language. With only 4.5 million others speaking it, they are well aware that to communicate with the world they must be the ones making the effort to learn other languages. German is usually the third language, although many also learn French in school. With increased travel to the warm and sunny resorts of Europe and beyond, English is usually the mediating language.

There is an expectation, however, that those who will will be staying in Norway for some time should learn the language to facilitate their integration. Free state-provided courses in Norwegian are available in the larger towns.

The major problem likely to be encountered by students of Norwegian is in finding the opportunity to practice their language skills. Ever helpful, Norwegians in shops, banks, and post offices will reply to a faltering Norwegian query with a response in perfect English!

One British engineer working on a Norwegian oil production platform, and determined to learn the language, found a novel way to get the practice he needed. He wore a printed sign on his helmet that warned all comers: *Jeg snakker bare norsk* (I speak only Norwegian).

JOINING CLUBS AND SOCIETIES

Norway abounds with clubs, societies, and associations. Indoor and outdoor recreations and sports provide opportunities for joining clubs: soccer, archery, rifle shooting, cross-country skiing, martial arts, and running, to name just a few. The country caters very well to outdoor activities and even the smallest communities have floodlit outdoor playing fields.

Choirs (both church and secular) are popular, as are groups for the encouragement of folk art, such as embroidery or *rosemaling* (wood painting). Norwegians are great joiners of professional associations and institutions; these organizations meet and hold seminars periodically.

Those with children often find the local school a focal point, becoming involved in organization or fund-raising for the school band or sports team.

EXPATRIATE ASSOCIATIONS

For those who want to meet people from their own culture, the towns with sizable expatriate populations offer good opportunities. There are large, formal organizations, such as the Oslo branch of the Federation of American Women's Clubs Overseas (FAWCO) or the Stavanger Petroleum Wives' Club, which has its own clubhouse with regular meetings and events. There are also informal gatherings of particular nationalities which meet for a chat. Find contact details through www.expatriates.com, your embassy Web site, or in local publications in your own language. International or British schools in Oslo, Bergen, Trondheim, Stavanger, and Sandefjord are also good starting points for English speakers, as are the Anglican chaplaincies and international churches.

chapter five

THE NORWEGIANS AT HOME

QUALITY OF LIFE

Although the great outdoors plays an important role in the lives of Norwegians, who spend as much time as possible in the open air, the focus of life is the family home and they tend to be very house-proud. Whether sophisticated and stylish or folksy-traditional, the overriding feeling is one of welcoming comfort.

Harsh winters are kept firmly outside by the use of effective insulating materials, and most modern houses are built in an open-plan design, which allows the heat to circulate. Wood burning stoves are popular and give off a very powerful heat. A woodpile stacked with logs is a common sight outside most rural and suburban homes.

With plentiful supplies of hydroelectric power, electricity is the fuel used for cooking and heating in Norwegian homes. Under-floor heating is very common, especially in hallways, bathrooms, and laundry rooms.

The garden is increasingly seen as an extension of the home and made much use of in the long, light hours of the summer months, when barbecues are popular. Spring flowers are very commonly planted in gardens and after such a long, hard winter the arrival of the snowdrop, followed by the crocus, then the daffodil, and lastly the tulip, is warmly welcomed. As soon as the slightest hint of spring is in the air, work on the garden begins, with the aim of having it looking good, preferably with an abundance of red tulips, for Norway's National Day on May 17.

Norwegians are very house-proud. Three British women, each married to a Norwegian for over twenty years, found they had suffered the same experience on moving to their husband's country as newlyweds. All had been informed in no uncertain terms that their cleaning efforts were less than adequate. Precise instructions on how to clean or *vask* (literally wash) the house were thoughtfully provided by their new mothers-in-law!

LET THERE BE LIGHT

In a country where the winter is long and dark, it is not surprising to find that Norwegians do all they can to bring light into their homes. Since the advent of effective triple glazing, the windows in the principal living rooms of modern homes tend to be very large, sometimes becoming whole walls of glass. Except in the most built-up of areas, where neighbors overlook one another, Norwegians almost never close their drapes. These may be elaborately designed in expensive fabrics, but they exist purely for ornamentation.

Rather than use a single overhead light, Norwegians like the ambience provided by several muted lamps and wall lights. Candles are also considered an important lighting medium, and there are some beautiful ones in the shops.

In the winter, and particularly in the Advent and Christmas season, burning candles are placed outside to welcome visitors, and special candlebridge lamps and electric stars are placed in the window as symbols of light in a dark world.

LIVING CONDITIONS

Over 60 percent of Norwegians are homeowners, with a further 13 percent part owners in housing cooperatives or similar schemes. Slightly less than a quarter of the population rent their homes and there is a small amount of municipal housing available for those who have problems managing to buy a home on the open market or who have special needs.

In the larger conurbations, particularly in Oslo,

housing arrangements are at variance with
the rest of the country. While nationally only
21 percent of the nation live in apartment blocks,
46 percent of Oslo's inhabitants are apartment
dwellers. In the larger towns accommodation
tends to be smaller and more cramped, but in
Norway as a whole housing is spacious by
European standards.

Much of the housing stock is modern: over 50
percent of dwellings have been built since 1970. In
areas of growth, such as the oil
town of Stavanger and its
suburbs, a great deal of building
is currently taking place, with
smaller semidetached and
terraced housing providing
opportunities for young people to
get a foot on the property ladder.

Almost two-thirds of the population live in
detached houses. It is common for these to be
three storied, with the basement partially
underground and housing the home's extra
facilities: laundry room, play room, perhaps guest
rooms, or a sauna. Depending on the size of the
property, it is not unusual for the basement floor
to be converted into a one- or two-bedroomed
flat (*leilighet*) or a studio apartment (*hybel*). These
separate dwellings are often rented out for
additional income or may be used to house the

extended family, for example grandparents or young marrieds.

LANDSCAPE AND ARCHITECTURE

Stone- or brick-built apartment blocks may be found in the larger towns, but traditional Norwegian homes are built of wood. Steep roofs

prevent snow from being a heavy burden on the structure. In past times grass roofs kept in warmth and were less vulnerable to the problems of snowfall: it is a novel sight on one of these old buildings to watch a goat scaling the roof, as it would a hillside, cropping the grass as it goes. Today shiny roof tiles encourage the snow off the roof as soon as possible.

Self-built housing is very popular in Norway. It is quite common for a young couple to rent an apartment while the home of their dreams (as far as their income allows) is being built. Individuals will do much of the building and laboring work themselves, calling on the help of friends and family, help that will be returned when needed by the next self-builder. In a country where there is an abundance of majestic scenery, homes are, wherever possible, built to take advantage of the views. Waterside vistas are especially coveted, and large numbers of Norwegians are fortunate to be able to enjoy these.

A HOUSE IN THE COUNTRY

Many Norwegians own a second home, the country cabin, or *hytte*. These are usually situated in the mountains or by the coast and provide a retreat from the workaday, technological world. If you are fortunate enough to be invited to a Norwegian's vacation home, then you are honored indeed, as this is their refuge from the world.

Sometimes the *hytte* is an old family home or farmstead, handed down from generation to generation; sometimes it has been more recently acquired and increasingly large numbers of new *hytter* are being built in the rural areas to satisfy the Norwegian desire to get back to nature.

The facilities provided in *hytter* vary enormously. Some Norwegians take their getting back to nature very seriously indeed. The original cabins had no running water, making use of wells, and a call of nature really was just that! Such people prefer to keep the *hytte* experience authentic by refusing to install any modern conveniences. They are disparaging about the growing number of people who desire some comfort in the vacation home, installing dishwashers, showers, flushing toilets, heated floors, and other luxuries.

RENT OR BUY?

As we have seen, the vast majority of Norwegian residents own their own home. Whether renting or buying in Norway, you will encounter the open market. Real estate agents *(eiendommegler)*, many of whom are linked to the banks, work for those both selling and renting property. Properties are advertised in their offices, in local newspapers, and on the Internet.

A large rise in property prices over recent years has created some problems, particularly for those wishing to buy their first property. In the larger towns, like Oslo and Bergen, housing is at a premium and prices are steep. In the rural areas prices are more affordable for obvious reasons.

Property may be rented unfurnished, or more commonly furnished, and longer leases are preferred. Rent is usually payable one month in advance, with a deposit of two months' rent standard practice. An inventory will be taken when you move in and both parties sign an agreement. When it is time to move out, it is worth remembering the Norwegian penchant for cleanliness. The property must be left spotless or the owner can charge a hefty fee for cleaning.

Mortgages to buy are arranged through the banks and a minimum deposit of 20 percent is usually required. Individual viewings of property are rare (unless it has failed to sell). Prospective buyers are invited to *visnings* (viewings), when information about the property, including surveyors' reports, will be available. Those seriously interested in the property after viewing leave their name and contact number. They will be called when someone has opened the bidding. A bidding war then takes place over a short period of time until the property is sold. Officially registering the purchase of the property costs 2.5 percent of the purchase price and there is also an official stamp duty payment.

THE NORWEGIAN FAMILY

The results of the Norwegian census of 2001 show that family size is decreasing. The average number of people per household is 2.3, compared with 2.4 in 1990, and 3.3 in 1960. The majority of families today have one, two, or three children and the larger families of yesteryear are all but gone.

Of the total population ages twenty and over, 62 percent live as couples, the vast majority of those being married. Only one-fifth cohabit, although when age is taken into account, those in the younger age bracket show a growing tendency toward cohabitation, 60 percent preferring that to marriage. The divorce rate in Norway is high, and there is a growing band of single parents. Six percent of all households consist of a mother or father with one or more children; 90 percent of these single parents are women. The rise in divorce has also led to an increase in the proportion of people living alone: today almost a fifth of the population, with the rates higher in the urban areas.

Although, in common with most developed countries, family size is decreasing and family composition is changing as a result of divorce and remarriage, the family is still at the center of Norwegian life. Family, old friends, and local roots are very important, and the majority of people still live in the community in which they were born, or maintain close ties there through parents, grandparents, or a second home.

DAILY LIFE AND ROUTINE

Norwegians tend to rise early as the working day begins at 8:00 a.m. for office workers, earlier for some industries, and at 8:30 a.m. for schoolchildren. Today packaged breakfast cereals served with milk or yogurt are popular, particularly with children, but a traditional Norwegian breakfast consists of bread with cheese, ham, or salami, topped by thinly sliced tomato or cucumber. Eggs—soft- or hard-boiled—are also popular. Juice and coffee or tea accompany the meal.

Primary children may finish their school day by 11:30 a.m. or noon, while secondary pupils are unlikely to be dismissed before 2:00 p.m. Many younger children stay on for extra activities or to attend the after-school club.

Despite the fact that the main meal of the day, dinner, is known as *middag* (literally midday), there is little tradition of eating a hot meal at lunchtime in Norway. There is no meal provision in schools and children must take a packed lunch. For a small monthly fee many companies offer their employees a subsidized cold, light lunch, which is eaten early, from about 11:00 a.m.

Throughout the day, strong black coffee is consumed. For most people the working day is usually over by

4:00 p.m., particularly in the summer months, and the hot evening meal is eaten early, between 5:00 and 6:00 p.m., or later if there are guests. The evening is the time for relaxation in the home or at one of the numerous clubs that Norwegians like to join. Sporting activity is also popular. The early morning start means that many are in bed quite early. This changes in summer when the long hours of daylight can play havoc with the sleeping patterns and, anyway, Norwegians want to make the most of the light. It is not unusual to hear children playing outside late in the evening at this time of the year.

ATTITUDES TO CHILDREN

Norway is a very child friendly society, but that does not mean that Norwegians mollycoddle their children, in fact, far from it. With the majority of mothers working, children tend to be independent from an early age. The young children of working parents may attend a kindergarten or nursery or spend the day with a *dagmamma* (registered day-care provider). The use of private nannies is not so common.

Although parents may accompany children when they start school, at age six, children soon make their own way there and back. It is virtually unheard of for children to be taken to school by car, as has become the custom in many other countries. In the towns and suburbs children have safe routes to school via pavements, cycle tracks, pedestrian crossings, bridges, and underpasses. Quite young children walk or cycle home and then look after themselves, playing and fixing themselves food if they are hungry, until their parents arrive home from work.

Norway has a reputation as a "safe" country, which means that children are granted much greater freedom to roam than in many other places, where parents fear danger on every corner. Road traffic in Norway is relatively light and speed limits, particularly in residential areas, are very low and controlled by speed bumps. Motorists should also be aware that children have the right to stop the traffic when they wish to cross by putting out their hand.

Leisure time is valued in Norway and children's play is recognized as important. Even small communities have good sports facilities and school playgrounds are well equipped with climbing apparatus and play equipment. Residential areas often have a wealth of children's designated play areas, with swings, slides, sandpits, wooden playhouses, rope slides, adventure cycle tracks, and skateboard areas. If a local hill is suitable for sledging, then the authorities will ensure that it is well lit to enable children to take full advantage of it.

Through adventurous play and freedom, Norwegian children acquire confidence and independence. Discipline tends to be quite low-key, and physically punishing children is strictly forbidden. Those from more punitive cultures should be aware that smacking, hitting, or hurting a child can result in imprisonment. Even raising your voice to a child in a public place may result in disapproving looks and acerbic comments.

EDUCATION

Many children make use of nursery or preschool provision in Norway. At this stage it takes the form of learning through play as formal teaching is not permitted by the education authority. This relatively long period of play-based learning, which extends into the first year of primary school, encourages teamwork and consensus, vital aspects of Norwegian socialization.

The ten compulsory years of schooling begin at age six. Seven years are spent in primary school and from ages thirteen to sixteen children enter the lower secondary level. During these years a broad and general

education, laid down in the National Curriculum, is undertaken. Children for whom Norwegian is a second language are provided with mother tongue tuition, where possible, by the state.

Where appropriate, some special curricula have been devised. For example, hearing-impaired children make use of Norwegian Sign Language as their first language. Sami children learn about their own cultural heritage, language, and identity. The strong principle of equality in Norway means that there are no single-sex schools. Children of all capabilities are integrated into the education system. Those with mental and physical disabilities, as far as possible, join normal classes. This teaches patience and acceptance of all, but can slow down the pace of the class and leave more academic pupils unchallenged and disruptive.

While extra help is offered to slow learners, the Norwegian principle of just enough for all and not standing out from the crowd means that gifted children, with their own special needs, are overlooked, an unfortunate by-product of the egalitarian system. This, together with a low-key attitude to discipline (pupils call their teachers by their first names) has led to growing concern by some parents, and an unprecedented drift toward the few private schools.

In primary school no marks or examinations

are given as it is believed that children do their best without pressure. Examinations taken at the end of the lower secondary level provide an indication of pupils' achievements and help to decide whether they—the majority of pupils remain in education at sixteen—move on to an academic, vocational, or combined course at *videregående skole* (upper secondary school).

In the more remote areas small schools may, of necessity, group children of different ages together at the primary and lower secondary levels. Such children may need to live away from home to attend upper secondary school.

Education stops being free at the higher level: Norway has four universities (Oslo, Bergen, Trondheim, and Tromsø) and twenty-six university colleges (*høgskoler*). However, tuition fees are reasonable and the State Educational Loan Fund provides student loans and grants for living expenses, which are also available to the many students who study abroad.

There are very few private schools in Norway. They may be authorized if they are religious or ethically based, if they provide tuition that is not available in the state school system, or if they employ alternative teaching methods, e.g., Montessori or Steiner. Their curriculum must be approved by the Ministry for Education and they are then eligible for government funding.

A Hardy Upbringing

Traditionally preschool day care took place outdoors in all seasons, even in the most northerly part of Norway. Children, well wrapped in their snowsuits, gloves, hats, and boots would play outside all day, only going inside for a short period at lunchtime. A few establishments, run on these principles, still exist today. At some, older preschool children are dropped off at the meeting house in the morning, sensibly clad for the day's activities and bearing a backpack containing lunch and a drink, and spend the day with their leaders exploring the outside world and learning about nature.

CHANGING LIFESTYLES

Inevitably the massive social change brought about by the rapid growth in prosperity since the discovery of oil thirty or so years ago is leading to changes in the traditional Norwegian lifestyle.

Norway's national character was forged by the challenge to survive in a difficult terrain and a hostile climate. Although climate and terrain may not have changed, the human ability to conquer or accommodate these difficulties has, and for most people, life, travel, and communication are unrecognizably easier than they were forty years ago.

Communities that may have viewed the inhabitants of the next valley as incomprehensible foreigners now watch Australian soap operas on satellite TV and fly to Thailand for their holidays.

Technology has enabled the growing influence of imported TV, music channels, and the Internet, which is leading to the globalization of the young, something happening in many nations across the world. The result can be that the young have more in common with youngsters on the other side of the world than they do with older citizens of their own country. Of course, it is to be hoped that this will have positive outcomes as regards world peace, but it does not augur well for the survival of the traditions of individual countries.

The number of immigrants in Norway is also growing. Membership in the European Economic Agreement has enabled other Europeans to live and work in Norway, but the need for large numbers of workers to support an aging population has led to further immigration, as has Norway's commitment to take its share of refugees and asylum seekers. The largest group of immigrants is from Pakistan, but Iraq, Iran, Somalia, Vietnam, and Turkey also figure among the highest intake. Among European immigrants, numbers from Bosnia, Serbia, Poland, and Russia are also high. The introduction of other cultures and religions influences the host country and, as we have seen, there are rumblings of disquiet and racial disharmony in some areas, particularly in the towns and industrial districts where immigrants are more likely to settle in order to find work.

Norway is one of the wealthiest nations in the world with arguably the highest standard of living, but there are signs that the very rich are growing richer faster than the rest of the population, leading to inequalities. Norway is not alone in seeing a growing drug problem in its larger towns, with a resulting increase in the crime rate. Some fear that the halcyon days are coming to an end and that Norway's relative innocence and "safeness" may be at risk. For many years, Norway's northern location and its immigration policy kept it comfortably isolated from all but its Scandinavian neighbors. The exploitation of Norway's oil fields has brought enormous wealth and rapid modernization, but becoming an important player in an international industry has also brought the big bad world to Norway's door and some feel this is proving to be a two-edged sword.

chapter six

TIME OUT

For most Norwegians a large proportion of leisure time is spent engaged in some outdoor activity. According to the season or the proximity to coast or mountain, this could involve hiking, cross-country skiing, boating, playing football, or just gardening. Socializing with small groups of friends and family is another important way to relax. Norwegians keep their homes and gardens well maintained and most entertaining takes place at home, with outdoor cooking and eating popular in the summer months.

Norwegian society recognizes the importance of leisure time for recharging the batteries of body and soul. Many would say that the work/life balance is weighted in favor of life. The working day ends promptly for most and overtime working is uncommon. Earlier closing times in banks, post offices, and some public offices during the summer months give maximum opportunity to enjoy free time. However, with high prices everywhere, the only problem may be affording the leisure pursuits on offer.

SHOPPING

On the whole, shopping is still viewed as a
functional exercise rather than a leisure pursuit.
The opening hours for shops vary, but the core
hours are 10:00 a.m. to 5:00 p.m. from Monday to
Friday, closing at 3:00 p.m. on Saturday. Recently
supermarkets have begun opening at 9:00 a.m.,
with the odd one opening earlier at about 7:30
a.m. Most supermarkets remain open until 8:00
p.m. Monday to Friday, closing earlier on
Saturday. Some town centers have late night
shopping on Thursday until 6:00 or 8:00 p.m.

With the exception of the occasional
convenience store, shops do not open on Sunday
or public holidays, although there may be a
limited amount of Sunday hours for Christmas
shopping in December.

High quality woolen knitwear features high on
the list of typical Norwegian products popular
with visitors. Wooden ornaments, particularly
those embellished with *rosemaling*
(traditional hand-painted
decorations whose styles and colors
vary from region to region) are also
widely available in towns and
tourist areas. Candles and
candlesticks abound as do
pewter (*tinn*) goods, often
with a Viking theme, and

hand-painted glassware. Silver jewelry is a good buy: there is a wide range from the most modern styles to traditional designs worn with the *bunad* (national costume).

USEFUL SHOPS	
Apotek	Pharmacy / Chemist
Bakeri	Bakery
Blomsterbutikk	Flower shop
Bokhandel	Book shop
Grønnsakhandel	Fresh fruit and vegetable shop
Helsekost	Health food shop
Jernvarehandel	Hardware store
Konditori	Pastry or cake shop
Matvarehandel	Grocer
Renseri	Dry cleaner
Supermarked	Supermarket
Vaskeri	Laundry

TAX BACK FOR TOURISTS

Value-added tax *(merverdiavgift)* (shortened to mva) of 23 percent is levied on all goods and services, with the exception of property, medical services, used cars, books, and some other items. (The rate of mva on food has recently been reduced.) The addition of mva, coupled with already high Norwegian prices, can make shopping an expensive experience for visitors.

Tourists from outside the Nordic region can receive a refund of between 11 and 18 percent of the sale price if they shop at stores displaying the "Tax Back for Tourists" sign. A minimum purchase of NKr 310 (about U.S. $50 or £26) is required and then tourists will receive a Global Refund Check. It is important not to unpack the goods before leaving the country. On departure from Norway present the Global Refund Check to the tax-free representative at the airport or ferry port to receive an immediate cash refund.

BANKS AND CURRENCY

Banks are open Monday to Friday from 8:15 a.m. to 3:30 p.m., with a late night on Thursday until 5:00 p.m. There are no weekend hours. ATMs are widely available.

The *krone* (plural *kroner*) is the Norwegian unit of currency. For international purposes this is written as NKr or NOK, but shops within Norway display prices as Kr. Although there are 100 *øre* in one *krone*, the tiny 50  *øre* is the only *øre* coin and is seen increasingly rarely. Prices in shops are tallied and then rounded to the nearest 50 *øre*.

Debit and credit cards are widely used in shops, restaurants, taxis, etc. You swipe your own card through the card reader and enter your PIN number. The message g*odkjent* informs you that your purchase is approved.

The most popular method for paying bills in Norway is via the giro form, which you fill in, sign, and take or send to a bank. Money is then automatically transferred from your account to that of the recipient.

EATING OUT

Norway has never been known for its *haute cuisine*, but things are definitely improving. Oslo and the larger towns offer a wide selection of restaurants, many of them excellent. Ethnic cuisine is also available in such places, as are café-bars, offering innovative menus. In rural areas and villages there will be less choice and you may have to rely on the hotel restaurant.

Norwegian cooking tends to be fairly plain, relying on meat or fish served with boiled potatoes and vegetables. Inexplicably, a salad made of shredded lettuce, canned sweet corn, and chopped cucumber and tomato doused in Thousand Island dressing seems to garnish every less expensive meal.

Pork is the most widely available and least expensive meat; beef and strongly flavored lamb or mutton are also available; poultry is still relatively uncommon. Many visitors take the opportunity to try elk or reindeer. Meat patties (*kjøttkaker*) and stews (*lapskaus*) with dumplings (*kømler*) are traditional hot, bulky meals to keep out the winter cold.

Fresh fish and seafood are of a high quality, particularly when simply prepared and served without overpowering sauces. Smoked salmon and prawns are always available in quantity. Vegetarians are unlikely to find themselves well catered to, particularly outside the main towns, and vegans are probably in for a very lean time.

Desserts are often a variation on crème caramel, jelly, or a light mousse served with evaporated milk. Berries are a real favorite, and truly flavorful blueberries and strawberries are abundant in the summer. Cloudberries (*multer*) are a coveted luxury. Most restaurants offer a full wine list, but prices are very high.

Lunch in Norway is usually cold, perhaps an open-faced sandwich (*smørbrød*), but the day's best offers are often available in restaurants at lunchtime. The *dagens rett* is the daily special, a meat or fish dish, served with potatoes and vegetables, and sometimes including a drink.

Hotel breakfasts are mostly included in a bed

and breakfast arrangement and usually involve a self-service table of bread, cheeses, eggs, cold meats, tinned or bottled fish, jams, and yogurts. Dinner in the better hotels, particularly in the mountains, will often offer an extensive *koldtbord* (cold table, similar to the Swedish *smørgåsbord),* groaning with an array of fish, meat, cheese, and egg dishes, accompanied by delicious breads, salads, and fruits. The meal should be started with fish and a clean plate used for each course. The art is to eat in a leisurely manner and make as many return trips to the table as necessary. Beer or *akevitt* (traditional liquor distilled from potatoes and grain) is recommended with this meal.

Eating out in Norway is expensive and, once you are outside the larger towns, roadside restaurants and cafés are rare. When traveling, or on excursions, the majority of Norwegians bring their own food and drink. It is not uncommon to see them picnicking in full foul-weather gear along the route or at popular recreation sites.

SERVICE
Norwegians in shops, banks, restaurants, and bars are polite and helpful enough, but if you are expecting anything beyond that then you will be disappointed. A culture of equality for all means that serving others has somehow become confused

with subservience, an undesirable quality. That, taken in conjunction with the plain-speaking manner of Norwegians, which can come across to outsiders as brusqueness, may leave you feeling you have been served with the minimum of courtesy.

Shop assistants may well finish their conversation before attending to you, supermarket checkout operators all but throw your purchases down the conveyor belt, and waiters take your order with barely a smile. The travel agent on the other end of the telephone line will tell you she cannot complete your booking now because it is 4:00 p.m. and she is going home. These people are not deliberately snubbing you: there is just little culture of service in the country.

TIPPING

Service is included in many restaurants, but where it is not, waiters would not expect to receive more than 5 percent of the bill. While taxi drivers do not expect a tip, fares may be rounded up to offer a few *kroner*. Porters at train stations and airports usually charge per piece of luggage, while hotel porters generally expect NKr20 for their help. You do not tip hairdressers or beauticians. Norwegians have a good standard of living: there is little incentive for them to put themselves out for you.

All in Good Time

A British family sitting in a restaurant in Stavanger became more and more impatient as they waited to be given menus to peruse. Finally, after ten minutes or so, a waiter wandered over to their table. "Can I help you?" he asked. When told that his customers would like to eat something, he seemed vaguely surprised. "We'd like to see the menu," they asked pointedly. "Oh sure," he replied casually and ambled off to find one.

While loud or aggressive behavior never works, it is sometimes necessary to make your demands known politely but firmly or you may be in for a long wait!

ALCOHOL

Attitudes to alcohol vary greatly among Norwegians and as a newcomer it may seem that everyone you meet is either a teetotaler or a very heavy drinker. There is still an active temperance society that from time to time runs visible campaigns promoting abstinence.

Drinking is on the increase among the young and is mostly visible as binge drinking on Friday and Saturday nights in the town centers. The high cost of alcohol in bars and clubs means that many youngsters consume most of their alcohol at home and so arrive at their drinking location already fairly "merry." Norwegians may be reserved but they do know how to party. Alcohol plays a large part in this and many newcomers may be surprised to find that bars and cafés become very lively as the drinks slip down and the Norwegians come out of their shells. Although town centers can be raucous on Friday and Saturday nights, the mood is generally merry rather than intimidating.

Beer is available in most supermarkets during licensing hours and will be curtained off outside of these. Wines and spirits may only be purchased in the state run *vinmonopol* stores, which also have restricted hours controlled by the local town or district council (*kommune*). As a result, availability varies quite widely throughout the country. As you might expect, alcohol is much easier to come by in Oslo and the other major towns than in rural areas.

The tax on alcohol is high and increases with the strength of the drink, so that spirits are almost prohibitively expensive. Bars only really exist in the towns and you are likely to pay NKr54 (about U.S. $8.75, £4.55) for a half liter (about a pint) of beer.

Home Brews

Helping to keep down the cost of your favorite tipple, home brewing is popular and many supermarkets sell kits to get you started on wine and beer making. Home distilling of liquor from sugar and potatoes is illegal but widespread in certain areas of the country. The strength of the liquor produced poses more dangers than you might imagine. An illegal still exploding in the basement has been responsible for the destruction of a considerable number of family homes.

SMOKING

Despite the generally healthy lifestyle, a surprisingly large number of Norwegians seem to be quite heavy smokers. Cigarettes and tobacco are expensive as a result of heavy taxation, so duty-free imports are highly prized and many roll their own cigarettes.

Since 2004 smoking has been banned in all public places. Workplaces must provide a designated outdoor smoking area and some restaurants and bars have covered outdoor areas for smokers. However, winter temperatures do not make this a tempting option for everyone!

S*nus* (chewing tobacco) is also widely available and has increased in popularity since the 2004 smoking ban. One in five *snus* users is female and over 50 percent of Norwegian tobacco chewers are ex-smokers, making the change for social and dubious health reasons. (Although *snus,* being smoke free, is not a cause of heart and lung disease, it is linked with oral cancers.)

HIGH CULTURE

Norway may be small in population, but it has a cultural heritage to be proud of. The years leading up to the dissolution of the union with Sweden saw a blossoming of Norwegian culture, highlighted by the achievements of the artist Edvard Munch, the playwright Henrik Ibsen, and the composer Edvard Grieg. The works of these cultural icons are celebrated to this day. State subsidies and the introduction of traveling theater companies aim to make the arts more available to all Norwegians. However, in practice, the arts are mostly accessed by a cultured minority in the major towns.

Oslo has a wealth of art galleries to suit all tastes: the National Gallery, Munch Museum, Museum of Applied Art, Museum of Contemporary Art, and the Astrup Fearnley Museum of Modern Art. The Vigeland open-air

Sculpture Park, which displays the statues of Gustav Vigeland in the Frogner Park, is also worth a visit. Den Norske Opera performs the works of traditional composers, such as Puccini and Mozart, at the Opera House, as well as more contemporary pieces, and Oslo's National Theatre not only showcases the work of the two great Norwegian playwrights, Ibsen and Bjørnstjerne Bjørnson, but also that of contemporary Norwegian writers.

Traditional crafts are celebrated at the Norwegian Folk Museum of Oslo, which combines indoor displays of folk art, furnishing, implements, and costumes, plus an extensive outdoor collection of traditional wooden barns and houses that have been transported from all over the country and rebuilt on site.

Further north, visit the ancient Nidaros Domkirke (cathedral) of Trondheim and the various museums of the town, while, just outside Bergen, Edvard Grieg's picturesque lakeside home, Troldhaugen, can be found, with a museum detailing his life and the simple cabin where he composed much of his music. A small concert hall also houses recitals of his work at certain times of the year. During the summer months there are daily classical concerts in Bergen, mainly dedicated to the music of Grieg.

Music, ballet, folklore, and drama are also

celebrated in Bergen's annual International Festival at the end of May, and in October Bergen hosts its annual contemporary art festival, Bergart. In fact, festivals of the arts are to be found across Norway throughout the year.

FESTIVALS AND EVENTS
Many of the cultural festivals and events that take place throughout Norway capitalize on the long summer nights associated with the Midnight Sun, or the long days of winter to give an added ambience. The tourist board's Web site, www.visitnorway.com, provides a comprehensive list and contact details.

Jazz, blues, rock, and folk music are celebrated all year-round. Oslo's annual Norwegian Wood rock festival, showcasing the talents of Norwegian and international artists, is a major summer event, but festivals of jazz, hosted in bars and cafés, take place across the country from the Arctic Circle to the sunny south. In January Spitsbergen (Svalbard) hosts the world's northernmost jazz festival, while Trad Jazz is held in Stavanger. Jazz festivals are also held in Voss in March, Stavanger, Bergen, and Balustrand in May, Kongsberg and Molde in July, and Oslo gets in on the act in August. Blues can be heard in

Lillehammer and in Bergen in April. Norway's largest folk music festival takes place in the west coast town of Førde, north of Bergen, with performers from all over the world. Most towns of any size have live music venues, from piano bars to concert halls, that are popular throughout the year. Chamber and church music festivals also take place in the main towns.

For international film festivals visit Tromsø in January (again the world's most northerly), Haugesund in August, or Bergen in October. Gay Pride is celebrated in Bergen in May and, if you are in any doubt about the Scandinavian sense of humor, drop in on the annual Great Norwegian Humor Festival in Stavanger in June, when comedy spills out from the indoor venues onto the streets. Stavanger also hosts a wine festival and a food festival (*Glad mat*). And just to prove there really is something for everyone, try the Cherry Festival at Lofthus on the Hardangerfjord, where the world championships in cherry stone spitting are held!

Winter festivals are held in many major centers and in February Holmenkollen, just outside Oslo, is the setting for the annual Ski Marathon, when intrepid cross-country skiers take to the snow for a 26-mile (42-km) challenge. In March, considerably further north, Europe's longest dogsled race of 620 miles (1,000 km) follows the old mail route across the Finnmarksvidda Mountain Plateau. Winter sports festivals and competitions take place throughout the first three months of the year in Lillehammer, Geilo, and Holmenkollen.

For a traditional Norwegian experience visit Kopervik's Viking Festival or the one-hundred-and-fifty-year-old fair in the town of Roros, which has been designated a Cultural Heritage Landmark by Unesco.

LEISURE

Norwegian free time focuses on outdoor life, particularly in rural areas. However, multiscreen cinemas, theaters, concert houses, and art galleries exist in all the main towns and there are a number of museums that appeal to families. The Oil Museum of Stavanger provides hands-on experience for all. In Oslo it is possible to see a variety of museums dedicated to Norway's history of great explorers: the Viking Ships Museum and the Kon-Tiki, Fram, and Maritime Museums.

Leisure is one of the areas in which the unsophisticated nature of Norwegian life is most evident. This can, of course, be part of its greatest charm, and it is a pleasure to realize that Norwegian children do not require sophisticated (and expensive) manmade adventure parks to entertain them and get them away from the television. However, advertised attractions may not meet all expectations. For example, a working farm, open to the public, may contain two sheep and a goat, a hay barn, and some rusting plowshares. Also note that most attractions will only be open between mid-June and mid-August, with perhaps some weekend hours during May and early September.

SPORTS

Norwegians tend to enjoy a healthy lifestyle and this is reflected in their love of sports, both indoor and outdoor. The majority of children participate in sports at some level and this enables the country to produce a relatively high per capita number of champions. Sports facilities are good in most areas.

As in most European countries, soccer is a major interest at both the spectator and player levels. The harsh winter climate means that in Norway it is played in the summer. The annual Norway Cup is an international soccer tournament for youngsters. Handball is also very popular with children and played in most schools, as is volleyball. Classes in the martial arts are offered at many community centers. In recent years golf has been a growing sport, with the number of golf clubs across the country increasing. Cycling, too, is popular and for the fittest The Great Challenge is a bicycle race from Trondheim to Oslo.

For those interested in running, the June Midnight Sun marathon in Tromsø is held at midnight, but more conventional starting times are available at the world's northernmost marathon at Spitsbergen (Svalbard). A more challenging course is offered at the Norwegian Mountain Marathon, while in the summer Extreme Sport Week in Voss provides international competition in skydiving, rafting, climbing, and paragliding, to name a few.

As would be expected, water sports, particularly fishing, canoeing, and sailing, are highly popular. Winter sports, including skating and of course skiing, are widely enjoyed.

SKIING

They say that Norwegians are born with skis on: skiing is certainly the most popular winter sport, if not a passion. The origins of skiing lie, of course, in necessity. Archaeological evidence suggests that Norwegians have used skis to get about in the snow for 4,000 years. Legends even tell of the Norse god and goddess of skiing, Ull and Skadi.

The Norwegian phrase for skiing is *å gå på ski*, literally to walk on skis, and for Norwegians this means cross-country skiing. This is the form of skiing that all Norwegians learn as it enables  them to make the most of thousands of miles of trails across the winter landscape, including the many frozen lakes.

It was just over a hundred years ago that interest in skiing as a sport began to develop. Downhill or alpine skiing (*slalom*) followed and spread to Chamonix in the Alps. Today the excitement of downhill skiing is increasingly popular, especially with the young, and there is a huge interest in snowboarding too.

Norway has twice staged the Winter Olympics, in 1952 and 1994, and regularly produces gold medalists. Today ski marathons and festivals are held in the major resorts throughout the winter. Holmenkollen, just outside Oslo, hosts an annual ski marathon, ski festival, and the world's largest ski competition for children.

THE GREAT OUTDOORS
Many Norwegians spend as much of their leisure time as possible in the great outdoors. Vast areas of the country are wild and unspoiled with

astoundingly beautiful scenery, so it is no surprise that weekends and holidays see large numbers escaping from the towns and suburbs.

Around a quarter of the population own a *hytte*, or country cabin, which enables them to spend more time getting back to nature. For many, it is the unsophisticated activities of walking and hiking in breathtaking countryside that offer a necessary refuge from the working world. Large numbers of Norwegians own their own boat and are able to take advantage of the thousands of miles of waterways that surround and cut into the country. Sailing and canoeing are popular activities, as is fishing.

Enshrined in law is the Norwegian's right of passage over uncultivated land, which allows them to roam pretty much at will. A deep respect for the environment enables this law to exist without exploitation or damage. For many it is the simple act of communing with nature that is the most magnetic appeal of the outdoor life.

Books and leaflets detailing walking and hiking routes in English are available in the tourist offices and some large bookshops. However, non-Norwegians should take the information with a hefty pinch of salt. A walk described by a Norwegian hiker as a two-hour ramble may take a mere mortal over four hours and feel as if Kilimanjaro has been scaled!

chapter seven

GETTING AROUND

Norway is not a vast country. In some places it is less that 5 miles (8 km) wide, but it is over 1,000 miles (1,600 km) long and its deeply indented coastline and large proportion of mountains mean that it is not the easiest country to get around. And high prices can make traveling something of a luxury.

A huge development program, involving the building of roads, bridges, and tunnels, has greatly improved communication routes across the country. Tunnels 15 miles (25 km) long blasted straight through mountains can take hours off a journey that would previously have wound its way along mountain roads, or involved a long alternative route during the winter, when severe weather closes many roads. The world's deepest subsea tunnels join island areas and spectacular bridges link tiny communities. While this great network of tunnels speeds up travel times, some Norwegians complain that it creates a race of underground travelers and removes the journey from the breathtaking scenery.

ID CARDS AND RESIDENCY

All Norwegians carry a national identity card, bearing their photograph as well as their unique *personnummer* (personal number). As Norway is a member of the European Economic Agreement area (EEA), nationals from the European Union (E.U.) and the European Free Trade Area (EFTA) have the right to live and work within its borders. This means entering the country without need of a visa and being permitted to stay for three months (providing they are able to support themselves during this period) without needing to register with the authorities. Although the authorities allow a stay of up to six months to find work, those wishing to remain in Norway beyond the initial three months must register with the police.

Work permits are no longer required for EEA nationals, but stays beyond three months must be legalized by the acquisition of a residence permit, applied for at the local police station. This is usually valid for up to five years and may be renewed after that period if necessary. It is the foreigner's equivalent of the national identity card with photograph and *personnummer*. It not only enables you to register for benefits, but will also be required by doctors, dentists, banks, and bureaucrats to prove your identity in various situations of daily life. Renewable one-year permits are usually granted to students.

Citizens of some other countries, including the U.S.A., Canada, and Australia, may also enter Norway without a visa and stay for three months. Others must make visa applications through the Norwegian embassy in their home country and it is forbidden for them to enter Norway with the intention of looking for work. There are stringent laws concerning those seeking work from non-EEA countries, who will need to have a firm offer of work and a residence permit before their arrival in Norway. Those offering specialist skills will have a greater chance of success.

CARS AND DRIVING
The Norwegian road network covers over 56,000 miles (90,000 km). In the south, the main towns are served by the E18 expressway, while the E6 or Arctic Highway runs the length of the country from the southern Swedish border, through Oslo, Trondheim, and Narvik to Kirkenes on the Russian border.

Although traffic around the populous areas is busy at times, on the whole Norway's roads are reasonably quiet and, the further north you travel, the emptier the roads. In rural areas it is possible to drive for miles without seeing another car.

Generally drivers are courteous and there is little use of the horn. Speed limits (see below) are relatively low and traffic in most areas flows freely.

Toll roads are common in Norway and the charge can range from NKr 10 to 300. Funds raised are used to help finance the building of new roads and tunnels. Low tolls (usually between NKr 5 and 10) are payable to enter many of the larger towns, such as Oslo, Bergen, Trondheim, and Stavanger. For convenience residents can purchase a small "brick," which is fitted onto the windshield and read by the toll machine each time you pass. You will be sent a bill when your prepayment has run out.

Many find that driving in Norway is a less stressful experience than in other countries, but it is important not to become too relaxed. Speed limits and laws concerning drunk driving are strictly enforced and punishments are severe.

Driver's Licenses
Drivers with valid driver's licenses issued by European Economic Agreement (EEA) do not need to acquire a Norwegian license, although

they may exchange their license for a Norwegian one if they wish. Drivers from other developed countries, including Australia, Canada, and the U.S.A., can exchange their license for a Norwegian license after passing a practical test.

Give Way to the Right

All expressways and major routes bear a priority sign: a yellow diamond. Traffic on these routes always has priority over traffic joining from side roads. However, all residential roads and many minor roads are not "yellow diamond" roads, which means that you must give way to traffic joining from junctions on the right. Be warned that traffic will come straight out from these junctions. In particular, look out for the "yellow diamond" signs with a thick black stroke through them where the priority changes from your road to the side road.

Winter Driving

The use of winter tires is compulsory. The majority of Norwegians use studded tires, but there has been a move to reduce their use, particularly in southern towns where snow is less frequent, since they damage the surfaces of roads, and the resulting dust has been linked to an increase in asthma. The use of thick winter tread has been encouraged instead. Many find, however, that only studded tires really do the job in icy conditions. Winter tires may be used only between November 1 and Easter Sunday unless weather conditions demand their use outside these times. Many drivers also carry chains if they are traveling in mountainous regions.

Considering the sparse population in rural areas and the problems associated with terrain and climate, it is remarkable that so many roads are kept open during the winter. However, many roads are closed for up to seven months of the year and it is important not to set out on a winter journey without checking first. Call the Road User Information Center (175) or check www.vegvesen.no. Conditions can change quickly and dramatically, so keep checking. Where roads are open but difficult, there may be some *kolonnekjøring* (convoy driving) led by a snowplow.

It is important that those unfamiliar with severe conditions appreciate the dangers and difficulties of driving in remote areas. Always carry blankets, food supplies, and a shovel, and if you are unfortunate enough to break down or run off the road, remain inside your vehicle.

One general rule of winter driving is to give way to those going uphill.

Drunk Driving

The only advice is, don't do it. Norway has the
strictest drunk driving laws in Europe and they
are stringently enforced. With an 0.20 ml limit, it
is recommended that no alcohol is taken for
twelve hours before driving. The tiniest trace of
alcohol in the blood will lead to severe
punishment: an on the spot fine, loss of license,
and possibly even imprisonment.

Random routine road checks take place
wherever and whenever the police deem it
necessary. Take a bus or a taxi home after drinking
and do not assume you are safe to drive the
morning after a heavy drinking session. It is not
uncommon to be stopped and Breathalyzed in the
morning. The police simply set up a roadblock
and test everyone passing through it.

Speed Limits

Speed limits are strictly enforced and, if broken,
on the spot fines, loss of license, or imprisonment
can result.

Residential Areas	Built-up Areas	Open Roads	Expressways
19 mph	31 mph	50 mph	56 mph
(30 km/h)	(50 km/h)	(80 km/h)	(90 km/h)

Accidents and Breakdowns

Norway's roads are relatively safe, with one of Europe's lowest rates of traffic accidents. It is not mandatory to telephone the police (112) in the case of an accident, but contact details must be exchanged with the other involved parties. To call an ambulance dial 113.

The Royal Norwegian Automobile Club (KNA) and the Norwegian Automobile Association (NAF) provide advice and information on all aspects of motoring and roadside assistance. *Viking* and *Falken* are the two principal roadside services.

DRIVING TIPS

- Drive on the right.
- Low-beam headlights must be used at all times (except when high beam is necessary)
- Seat belts are compulsory front and rear.
- Always carry your driver's license, vehicle registration details, and certificate of insurance.
- Give way to the right on minor roads.
- Give way to children crossing.
- Red warning triangle compulsory.
- In rural areas watch out for animals, particularly at dusk.

AIR TRAVEL

The nature of the terrain means that air travel is common in Norway, and there are more than a hundred airports in the country, several of them international. Road travel between Stavanger and Oslo, for example, takes at least eight hours in the summer when the mountain roads are open, but flying time is around thirty minutes.

Regular flights to Norway's main towns depart daily from the major airports of Europe. Scandinavian Air Lines (SAS) is the principal domestic operator and Norway's main airport is Gardermoen, outside Oslo. Transportation (by express bus or train) is generally good between Norway's main airports and the towns they serve.

In a nation where transportation is impeded by mountain and fjord, air travel is as common as bus and train travel in other countries. Many Norwegians commute daily by plane to Oslo and other major towns and a simplified check-in system means that taking the plane is almost as easy as getting on the bus. Air travel is not cheap, but there are discounts for regular travelers.

TRAINS

Travel by train is a very pleasant, if expensive, way to see cross-country Norway. Norwegian trains, which are operated by the state railway company Norges Statsbaner (NSB), are clean, comfortable, and punctual. There are a few branchlines, but the three main routes connect Oslo to Stavanger, to Bergen, and to Trondheim, following on to Bodø in the north. NSB operates some bus routes to take the traveler on as far as the North Cape. Local commuter lines connect Oslo with its outlying towns.

Some of the routes through the mountains are worth experiencing for the amazing feats of engineering they represent. Others offer spectacular scenery: the route from Oslo to Bergen is particularly popular with tourists.

First- and second-class tickets are available and on longer journeys seat and sleeper bookings (for one, two, or three berth cabins) are compulsory. Tickets are not cheap, although the longer the journey, the more economical they tend to become. Concessionary fares are available (under fours are free, under sixteens and senior citizens pay half price), and there are family and group reductions. Special promotional prices exist from time to time.

On long-distance travel, don't expect conversation with your fellow passengers. Norwegians don't talk to complete strangers, so your journey is likely to be a silent one.

BUSES, STREETCARS, AND UNDERGROUND

Take the bus for a slower but more inexpensive way to travel. Buses take over where the rail track runs out and are a particularly good way to see fjordland Norway. Prices include the cost of ferry travel, which is a standard part of the journey in this area of Norway. The NOR-WAY Bussekspress company operates long-distance services the length of the country, into Sweden and Finland and as far south as Hamburg. Local operators run services between one town and the next.

All towns and most communities of any size will have a local bus service. Buses are usually clean and modern, and bus stops display timetables. Tickets are bought on board. Many large towns offer a skeleton *nattbuss* (nightbus) service on weekends. Local bus travel will also incorporate ferry travel where necessary.

Oslo's transportation system is efficient and comprehensive, with a network of streetcars, buses, and underground trains that crisscross the city from early morning until midnight. The central hub is Oslo Sentralstasjon, known as Oslo S, from which most of the city's routes fan out. (This is also a good place to obtain information about local and national travel.)

The underground, or the T-bane (Tunnelbanen), usually known simply as the "T," which is how its stations are marked, has eight lines that traverse the city and also run out into the fairly distant suburbs.

The usual concessionary fares apply to bus, tram, and underground travel, but travel passes are also a good buy, particularly in Oslo.

BOATS AND FERRIES

You can't travel far in Norway without encountering a ferry. Most are roll-on, roll-off car ferries that are regarded as part of the road system, and there is no need to book ahead. Journeys may take a few minutes or a couple of hours, in which case a cafeteria is provided. Ferries run fairly frequently on the busy routes, but if you want to avoid waiting, pick up a timetable. From May to September, when all of Norway seems to be on the move, waiting in line may be unavoidable.

In the towns many commuters regularly use the ferry shuttle services that cross waterways like the Oslofjord.

Particularly popular along the west coast around Bergen and its nearby fjords are the *hurtigbåt* passenger express catamarans. This is a fast but expensive option that can be rather unforgiving in choppy conditions. Ferry routes also link Norway with the UK, Germany, Denmark, and Sweden.

Probably Norway's most famous boat trip is the Hurtigrute or Coastal Express, which travels the route from Bergen to Kirkenes. This is a working ferry that stops at over thirty ports along the way and so short hops can be taken between ports. However, most visitors view this as an eleven-day cruise into the Arctic Circle along Norway's spectacular coastline. Fares are not cheap, but for many it is a once-in-a-lifetime experience, well worth saving up for.

TAXIS
Licensed taxis (*drosjer*) are available from stands in town centers or outside main stations and airports, or they can be booked over the telephone. Many companies now have an automated calling system. This recognizes the telephone number and address of the caller and then gives the option of pressing 1 for a taxi to be sent right away or 2 to be put through to an operator to arrange a taxi for later. For booked taxis you will always be given a booking number.

Taxis are expensive, but most fares are metered and drivers accept payment by credit or debit card. Service is included in the charge and, as we have seen, it is not usual practice to add a tip.

CYCLING

Although there is a limited amount of cycle track in and around the main towns of Norway, most cyclists take to the minor roads, which tend, as a rule, to be low in traffic volume. Cycling is popular with adults and children alike.

Bicycles can be rented in most tourist destinations. They generally go free on ferries but incur a fee on trains and buses. Cyclists are forbidden in the longer mountain tunnels as the fumes pose a serious danger to health. In these areas you will often find that the old pre-tunnel road is suitable for cycling.

The wearing of cycle helmets is not compulsory, but most people have the sense to wear them.

WHERE TO STAY

With high salaries and high taxes, the cost of hotel accommodation in Norway can be astronomical. However, with a wide range of accommodation available, from first-class hotels in town or mountainside to humble lakeside cabins, there is something to suit all tastes.

Hotels vary in size and the degree of comfort and amenities offered, but as a rule are clean and efficient. While the more costly hotels, particularly in Oslo and the mountain resorts, are often individual in their charm and style, budget priced hotels tend to be uninspiringly uniform. A buffet breakfast is always included in the room price and in some establishments this really can be quite a feast. While prices are high Monday to Thursday, there are often excellent discounts for weekends and the summer holiday period.

Those looking for something more individual should consider the *pensjonater* (pensions) or *gjestehus* (guesthouses), generally found in towns and tourist areas. The standard of amenities varies; at the top of the range rooms will have en suite facilities, at the lower end there will be a shared bathroom.

For an even more personal experience on the outskirts of towns and in the rural areas, many people offer a room in their homes to travelers. Look out for the Rom sign. Again, the standard will vary. Breakfast may be included, or kitchen facilities provided.

Those looking for basic budget accommodation, especially in fjordland Norway, should consider one of the one hundred hostels (*vandrerhjem*). In addition, some colleges offer rooms during the summer holidays. This can be an excellent way to get cheap, clean accommodation in or around the larger towns.

To those wishing to get closer to nature, one of Norway's hundreds of campsites, many in idyllic waterside locations, may appeal. Once again, size and amenities vary from just a field to pitch your tent to a large, well-appointed site.

If you wish to rough it, remember that it is "everyman's right" to camp one night in open uncultivated land, providing one does not cause harm or damage. As a matter of courtesy, to stay longer or camp with a large group, request permission from the landowner.

For a truly Norwegian experience, rent a lakeside or mountain *hytte* (wooden cabin), and to be really authentic rent one without "mod cons"!

The network of mountain huts dotted along the main hiking routes provides basic accommodation for hikers and cross-country skiers. Not all huts are staffed. In unstaffed huts leave payment in the box provided.

Information on *overnatting* (accommodation) in Norway can be found on www.visitnorway.com, or else see the individual Web sites of towns and tourist areas. The Norwegian Mountain Hiking Association (DNT) is a valuable resource, and can be found on www.turistforeningen.no.

HEALTH AND SECURITY

Norway is a safe country and the majority of
people you meet are courteous and helpful.
However, it is common sense not be complacent
about personal security, particularly in Oslo and
the larger towns.

Emergency Telephone Numbers	
Fire	Dial 110
Police	Dial 112
Ambulance	Dial 113

Norway's health service is state funded, and all
Norwegian residents are automatically covered. A
small fee is paid at point of service by those
between the ages of seven and sixty-seven.
However, there is an annual payment ceiling.
Once this has been reached the patient receives a
card that entitles the holder and any dependents
to free treatment for the rest of that calendar year.

The facilities of Norway's
national health service are available
to all E.U. nationals. E.U. members
should present an E111 form (soon to
be replaced by a card) to receive free
emergency treatment and hospital
inpatient care, or nonhospital treatment at a

reduced fee. Foreign visitors from non-E.U. states should take out medical insurance before departure. Prescriptions are filled at the *apotek* (pharmacy). Again, there is an annual payment ceiling. A late-night pharmacy will operate in most populated areas.

The medical facilities are modern and most doctors and therapists speak English. Hotels, taxi drivers, and tourist offices can direct you to the nearest hospital. For emergency treatment, visit the *legevakt* department of the hospital or doctor's clinic. After-hours dental treatment is available in the major towns.

Useful in an Emergency	
Doctor(s)	Lege(r)
Dentist(s)	Tannlege(r)
Hospital	Sykehus
Emergency Room	Legevakt
Pharmacy	Apotek
Prescription	Resept

chapter eight

BUSINESS BRIEFING

Traditionally Norway's economy was based on farming, fishing, and its offshoot industries—shipping and canning, for example. Compared with other European countries, Norway came late to industrialization. However, since the

war years there has been huge development of the manufacturing and technology industries. The finding of oil in the late 1960s and the subsequent growth of the oil industry have completely transformed the country, and this industry now dominates the economy.

A strong sense of self-sufficiency has always been part of the Norwegian psyche and is in part responsible for the country's rejection of membership in the European Union. However, the small population and a growing and successful economy meant that foreign workers were needed. As these flowed into the country and the influence of international companies grew, particularly in the oil industry, Norway began to take a more international approach. Signing the European Economic Agreement (EEA) has brought Norway more into line with its European neighbors.

Today you will find English widely spoken in the business environment. This, coupled with the growing international flavor of many companies, has made doing business with this wealthy nation much easier. However, Norwegian business has its idiosyncrasies, and it is advisable to be aware of them.

THE OFFICE

The atmosphere in a Norwegian office tends to be informal. The open-plan design is widely favored and, in some of the larger companies, there are no individual offices at all, even for the upper echelons of management. Meeting rooms are available for use when necessary. This, of course, corresponds to the principle of equality for all.

There is a strong culture of transparency and accessibility. An open-door policy exists for all staff as regards access to the highest levels of management. Titles are rarely used, but first names are. Dress is casual, with many employees coming to work in jeans and T-shirts or sweaters. However, casual does not mean outrageous. Conservative and functional tends to be the rule.

Black is a popular color choice and it would be unusual to find female workers turning up scantily clad. An important business meeting might instigate the wearing of a shirt and jacket, but suits and ties are never worn.

Norwegians are very fond of the high-tech trappings of business life. Mobile phones and handheld personal computers are everywhere. Business cards also play an important part in working life. Everyone has a business card, which will includes all contact details, including home telephone numbers.

Many successful businessmen in Norway are multilingual and it is not uncommon for them to have studied overseas. As in many societies, the upper spheres of business tend to know one another, forming a network that lives in the same areas and belongs to the same clubs.

WORKING HOURS AND TIMEKEEPING
The office day begins at 8:00 a.m., generally speaking, and ends on the dot of 4:00 p.m. In some towns, for example the oil town of Stavanger, there are large numbers of workers who fly in for the week. This is a result of the close links that Norwegians have with their home community, family, and school friends. To obtain the job of their choice these workers are willing to

work away from home, but not to relocate their family to a new town and leave behind friends and extended family. Such workers will often start early and leave late to make up the hours, which gives them greater flexibility for time at home.

The working day, Monday to Friday, is seven and a half hours, broken by a half hour lunch break. The lunch break is staggered throughout the company, but starts early, from 11:00 a.m.

The working week is thirty-seven and a half hours and overtime is rare and carefully regulated. There is generally a suspicion of overtime, the feeling being that someone who is efficient and capable should be able to finish their work during the official working day. In addition, law dictates that overtime must be paid at time and a half, which makes it less attractive to employers. The additional tax that payment at time and a half will incur makes it less attractive to employees.

Norwegian workers get twenty-five days paid leave each year and ten paid public holidays. However, where a public holiday falls on a weekend, there is no day off in lieu. If December 25 and 26 fall on Saturday and Sunday, with New Year's Day the following Saturday, there will be no time off at Christmas. This does not necessarily mean, however, that a lot of work will be done at this festive time!

The holiday period that does virtually close down Norwegian business is Easter (*Påske*). Maundy (Holy) Thursday, Good Friday, and Easter Monday are all public holidays. However, the school term ends on the Friday prior to Good Friday and, in practice, most people take the whole week leading up to Easter as vacation.

The summer vacation period runs from mid-June to mid-August, when the schools are closed for eight weeks. Workers are entitled to take three consecutive weeks off during the summer vacation. Everyone may take the weeks they wish, regardless of which weeks their fellow workers are taking. It is not permitted to deny them their choice in order to keep a business covered during the vacation period.

In addition, the *vinter ferie* (winter holiday) week, when the schools close midterm, usually in February and staggered across Norway, is a popular time for skiing.

COFFEE ON TAP
There is no coffee break, since drip (filter) coffee is available all day. It is drunk strong and black, sometimes with sugar but never with milk.

On the occasion of a special birthday with a zero on the end, or on their retirement, workers may treat their colleagues to a celebratory cake. In this case work will stop mid-afternoon!

LUNCH BREAKS

The half-hour lunch break is staggered within the company and starts from 11:00 a.m. In some large companies a cafeteria offers hot food, but there is little tradition of eating a hot meal in the middle of the Norwegian day, and a light buffet of bread, cheese, cold meat, and fish, with salad and fruit, for which workers pay a small monthly fee, is the usual provision.

BUSINESS ENTERTAINMENT

Business entertaining never takes place at home. It is not Norwegian policy to mix work and home life. Likewise, the business lunch does not really exist. In fact, taking a business guest out for a meal is not general practice. There is little tradition of eating out and the cost, particularly if the meal is supplemented with wine and other drinks, can be prohibitive.

Business entertaining is more likely to take place at an arranged event. A company may take advantage of the town's annual jazz festival, for

example. It will hire a suitable
venue complete with jazz
band, supper, and drinks, and
invite all their clients. This
way they can reward their
loyalty without favoritism.

Anything that could be viewed
as an inducement is seriously frowned
on in Norwegian business life. Some companies
send a letter at the start of the business year,
reminding contractors that gifts are not
acceptable. All gifts have to be declared and are
taxable. Where gifts are received, for example at
Christmas, they will often be pooled and shared.

TRADE UNIONS

Around three-quarters of Norwegian workers are
members of a trade union. The unions essentially
divide along occupational grounds, with separate
central organizations for blue-collar, white-collar,
and academic/professional workers. These
organizations are, in turn, centralized under the
Landsorganisasjonen (LO), the Norwegian
Confederation of Trade Unions. Blue-collar
workers make up more than half of trade union
members, and academics and professionals the
second-largest group, with almost one-quarter of
the membership. Women are more likely to join a

trade union and dominate the academic and professional union membership, where a substantial 76 percent of members are female.

There has been declining recruitment and membership over recent years and some areas of industry, such as the IT sector, show a reluctance on the part of employers and employees to welcome trade unions into the workplace. Unions are working to find new ways to attract the modern worker.

On the whole relationships between trade unions and employers are good. Unions play an active part in company decisions and are entitled to request up to one-third representation by the labor force on the board of directors. Union officials are also often involved in the hiring and firing of staff.

Trade union membership is voluntary and there are no restrictions on membership—no worker is denied the opportunity of joining a trade union because of their line of work. Closed shop agreements are generally not permitted.

WORKFORCE DISPUTES AND LABOR LAW
The strength of the labor and trade union movements in the postwar years has meant that Norwegian workers are well protected. The Working Environment Act dictates employment

conditions, the rights and responsibilities of employees, and the obligations of employers. Dismissal can occur as the result of the company's circumstances, for example a decline in productivity, or the employee's misconduct. Depending on the length of service, a fairly lengthy notice period at full pay may ensue. Employees have the right to challenge unfair dismissals through the Directorate of Labor Inspection. In practice, the labor laws favoring the workers and the no-blame culture mean that it can be difficult to dismiss an employee and it is often easier to buy out their contract than to try to dismiss them through the normal channels.

Main settlements regarding salary and conditions (usually on an industry-wide basis) take place every other year. Following a period of negotiation, two-year agreements are signed. As a result, the years with main settlements have many more disputes and work stoppages than the midterm years. For example, in 2002 (a main settlement year) 151,000 workdays were lost in connection with labor disputes. The following year only 1,000 days were lost, 57 percent of those in the oil industry. Residents in Norway become resigned to the biannual settlement period. The bus does not turn up and there are no trucks on the road for a couple of days. Usually disputes are resolved fairly quickly.

Where agreement cannot be reached between the Norwegian Confederation of Trade Unions (LO) and the Confederation of Norwegian Business and Industry then the dispute is referred to arbitration.

MANAGEMENT MODEL

As one might expect, organizations tend to be nonhierarchical. Status and position are not of prime importance. Employees like to think of themselves as the equals of their bosses, and as members of a team. First names are used in the office and heavy-handed management styles do not go over well. Management by intimidation is not part of the Norwegian way of life, and the workers do not live in fear of their superior. Norwegians simply do not respect someone who attempts to lay down the law by shouting and foot stomping. They think such a person has made a fool of themselves.

There is a sense of shared responsibility in Norwegian businesses. Individuals rarely make decisions. It is the role of the group or team to make a decision, often after many meetings and much discussion. As a result, they operate with a no-blame culture. If a mistake is made, it is made by the company, not by an individual, and the company will put it right. While an individual may be challenged on the issue within the company, it would be very unusual for anyone to lose their job for making a mistake.

Team Building

Teamwork is highly valued in Norway. From their earliest school experiences, Norwegians learn to cooperate. Those who engage in unacceptable behavior are not so much punished as ignored and excluded. They learn that to be part of the team is to be accepted.

Norway is not a highly competitive society, and this is reflected in the workplace. Managers see their role as coordinating the agreed upon

 activities of their team rather than imposing their way upon the workers. A great deal of time may be spent in planning the team response to a project or proposal, but once it is agreed upon, all members of the team are judged competent to play their part without heavy supervision.

Importance is placed on team-building activities, the majority of which will involve sports. Many companies own a cabin in the mountains and it is quite common for a manager to take their team there for a couple of days. Depending on the time of year, activities could

include canoeing, skiing, or orienteering. Unlike
the British model, where teams attend a
residential course run by specialist staff, the
Norwegian team-building experience is much
more informal and likely to be organized
in-house by the company ski or canoe expert.

THE GLASS CEILING BROKEN?

The high profile of women in politics gives
foreigners the impression that Norwegian women
have achieved a position of strength and equality.
Compared to a great many countries, they have,
but there are still major discrepancies between the
number of women in the workforce and the
number of women in executive positions. Women
constitute almost half Norway's workforce but few
hold key jobs in business and industry. Statistics
show that women executives are still a rarity, they
earn less than men, and their salary growth is
slower. "I've reached the glass ceiling and can go
no further. With regard to board positions, these
are based on whom you know. Men have a
network. They do not select on the basis of
whether you are competent or not, but on
whether they trust you and know you." So a
woman executive told the newspaper *Aftenposten.*

The Gender Equality Act of the 1980s brought
in comprehensive legislation to enhance the

position of women in all aspects of Norwegian society. The "60/40 rule" states that all public committees with more than four members must be made up of at least 40 percent females. Now the boards of private companies are being strongly encouraged to follow suit.

Public organizations have led in the advancement of women, and where women are in managerial positions they are unlikely to have to convince their Norwegian male colleagues of their seniority since they are used to the idea of equality. Women in the office will likewise not expect their male colleagues to open a door for them (though they may be pleasantly surprised if a foreign male shows them this courtesy).

BOARD MEETINGS AND DECISION MAKING

It is a legal requirement for limited (AS) companies to hold four board meetings a year, which must be fully documented. It is the job of the *daglig leder* (general manager) to call board meetings, and put together an agenda and the documentation necessary for the meeting to run as smoothly as possible.

The board consists of the board members (who are shareholders), the general manager (who may or may not be a shareholder), and the *styresmen,* "steersmen," or expert advisers. The steersmen are not members of the board, but are there to assist the general manager—for example, as an accountant or a legal compliance officer. As their title suggests, they help the meeting to stay on course. Only board members are allowed to vote.

Meetings, whether board meetings, team meetings, project meetings, or management meetings, play a very important role in the Norwegian working world. As confrontation is so difficult for Norwegians, decisions are made through consensus. This is particularly evident in the business context, where agreements are reached through discussion and compromise rather than through argument or straight voting.

This may take some time as every aspect and point of view must be discussed and it can be a lengthy process moving things forward. If agreement is not reached by the end of the working day, then it is not usual to carry on into the evening. 4:00 p.m. is 4:00 p.m! The meeting must resume tomorrow.

The desire to avoid confrontation means that foreigners will often be left puzzled when a business meeting which seemed to go well brings no concrete results. Rather than openly reject an offer or idea, the Norwegian may simply not return phone calls, e-mails, or correspondence.

> ### *TIME AND PLACE*
> A visiting British businessman, taking part in his first meeting with Norwegians, was amazed when on the dot of 4:00 p.m. the secretary who was taking notes closed her notebook, got up, and left. Her colleagues showed no surprise, and soon brought the meeting to a close. When the British visitor commented on this unprofessional behavior, he was informed by the secretary's manager that she had her children to collect, and so of course had to leave.

PRESENTATIONS

The style of presentations in Norway tends to be plain, unembellished, and straight to the point. Honesty is a key value and exaggeration of what is being offered is not welcome. In fact, it is not uncommon for Norwegians to point out certain weaknesses or disadvantages of the product or service they are offering. This is an indication of  their honesty and they value it in others. What will be appreciated is a well-researched, precise presentation, backed up with charts, figures, and analysis. Facts, benefits, and profitability should be emphasized.

Norwegians are very polite. As members of an audience, they will raise their hands if they wish to make a point or ask a question, so it is wise to leave time for questions and answers at the end of a presentation. Likewise, they will consider rude any interruptions to themselves while speaking. They will never be aggressive or confrontational if they disagree with aspects of what you are presenting.

Today, with the increase in the international workforce, a great many presentations are carried out in English.

NEGOTIATION

Negotiation discussions are frank and to the point. General chatting and joking are not part of any meeting. Once again, discussion will go on until agreement is reached, but bargaining and haggling are not part of Norwegian strategy. The preference for straightforward, plain speaking is evident. Quite often the Norwegians will open negotiating discussions with their final offer. Likewise, if they tell you that your product is too expensive they probably mean it. Norwegian companies are willing to pay for quality, and they will also readily switch suppliers to get better terms or higher quality. They are unlikely to be impressed by something just because it is "new."

Novel concepts will only be accepted if they have been demonstrated to be of high quality, practical, and well-tested.

Decisions are consensus driven. Although top managers make the decisions, they will be unlikely to ignore the recommendations of project leaders or middle management. Decision making may take some time as all the alternatives are carefully weighed. Above all, high pressure sales tactics are to be avoided. They will not work in Norway. Norwegians value an honest portrayal of what is on offer. They are suspicious of exaggerated claims and if goods or services do not meet the promises made, business relationships are likely to sour very quickly.

Many large companies, particularly those working internationally, may have British or American negotiators.

CONTRACTS AND FULFILLMENT
Once a contract has been agreed upon then it is imperative that you adhere to deadlines and commitments. Norwegians are punctilious about each point in the contract and it is not only your business relationship that will sour if you fail to live up to your promises. Although large companies may bring in lawyers to ensure that contracts are watertight, the law of the land is also

very clear that contracts should be followed to the letter. For example, usually thirty days' grace is given to pay a bill. Those that are not paid within that time attract an automatic, daily escalating fee.

Yet again, honesty is vital. It you do not stick to your proposals then you will be deemed untrustworthy and Norwegians will lose interest. It cannot be stressed too strongly that it is important not to overpromise at the negotiation stage. Making changes or additions will not be appreciated once an agreement has been reached and it is very difficult to renegotiate terms.

Contracts in the Norwegian Oil Industry

Companies wishing to hire work or services will consult a database known as Achilles to check for capable subcontractors. All serious contenders will be listed. Several will be invited to present. Formal presentations of services will be given to a company team. The team decision is very important as no one person may be seen to shoulder responsibility for any decision — an example of the no-blame culture. A review will then be carried out, possibly several reviews, before an invitation to tender is issued. A minimum of three companies will be invited to bid. The decision process can be extensive, but once a decision has been made, work is expected to commence immediately.

Contracts are legal documents governed by
Norwegian law, but drafted in either Norwegian,
English, or both. They are generally well drafted
and applied to the letter, with protracted
negotiations necessary to carry out any changes.
Again, it will require more than one person to
accept these changes, usually an engineer with
contract responsibility, his or her immediate
supervisor, and an accountant.

Generally a five-year contract has an escalation
rate built into it. This is based on the rate of
inflation (*konsumerprisindeks*) issued by the
Central Bureau of Statistics (*Statistisk Sentralbyrå*).
The figure is usually multiplied by a constant to
give 90 percent of the inflation figure, so a long
contract must be carefully priced to avoid erosion
by inflation. Payment of bills is generally within
thirty days, with interest added thereafter.

ESTABLISHING A BUSINESS IN NORWAY

The Norwegian economy relies heavily on
international trade and the government welcomes
foreign investment, allowing foreign investors to
own up to one-third of a Norwegian industrial
company. Joint ventures with Norwegian
companies are also encouraged.

Before establishing a business in Norway, a
foreign investor will need to obtain the

appropriate permits from the Ministry of Industry. Permits state that Norwegian labor and materials must be given preference. Foreign labor may only be used to provide skills that cannot be found in the Norwegian workforce. The local authorities must be approached regarding the use of premises and all new businesses must be registered with the Register of Companies (*Foretaksregisteret*), which will incur a registration fee, and also with the tax and social security departments.

Norwegian residents wishing to start a business may find it difficult to raise money outside Norway. Norwegian banks will give short- or medium-term loans to foreign businesses but for long-term investment it may be necessary to seek private investors. A detailed business plan with information on projected cash flow and repayment terms will be required at the time of application.

The Norwegian government offers various incentives to foreign investors in the shape of loans, grants, and advice through the Regional Development Fund (*Distriktenes Utbyggingsfond*) and the Small Business Fund (*Småbedriftsfondet*).

Those intending to take on employees will need to familiarize themselves with Norway's rigid labor laws, as well as the ever-changing complications of the tax system. It is vital to take advice from professionals.

chapter nine

COMMUNICATING

LANGUAGE

In this land of 4.5 million inhabitants, it is often said that there are 4.5 million dialects. While this may be rather an exaggeration, the isolation of communities caused over the centuries by terrain and climate has resulted in many different dialects, largely descended from the ancient Norwegian language.

In the spirit of national feeling in the years following the split from Denmark, it was decided to reduce the Danish influence by reclaiming the Norwegian language, replacing many Danish words with Norwegian dialect ones. Then, in the early part of the twentieth century spelling reforms took place so that the written language conforms closely with the spoken version, making spelling a much easier task for Norwegian children than their English speaking counterparts. Today, when new words are absorbed into Norwegian from other languages, such as English, the spelling is changed to bring it in line with Norwegian rules.

In fact, there are two official languages, *bokmål* (literally book language) and *nynorsk* (new Norse), both of which have equal status in official use and in education. *Bokmål* has traditionally had more social prestige and is the language of Norway's great literary figures. However, in practice, there is not a huge difference between the two languages. *Bokmål* is the language taught in most schools and is used in the majority of newspapers and television broadcasts. Many people write in *bokmål*, but speak *nynorsk*.

In the north, the Sami people have their own language, which is used and taught in primary schools. Sami belongs to the Finno-Ugric branch of the Uralic family, closely related to the Baltic Sea–Finnish languages, such as Finnish and Estonian. Unesco has classified it as an endangered language.

Norwegian is a Germanic language, similar enough to Swedish and Danish for most Scandinavians to be able to understand each other without too many problems. During the years of the Viking invasions, in the eighth and ninth centuries, English was influenced by the Norse language. In fact, English is closer to Norwegian than first seems obvious. Norwegian places consonants together in a way that could not easily be pronounced in English. It also has three additional vowels sounds, placed at the end of the alphabet: æ, ø and å. The Norwegian word *kjølig* looks unpronounceable to an English speaker but is actually pronounced shurly and means chilly; not so very different after all.

Fortunately for most English speakers, almost all Norwegians under retirement age will speak English, often with great facility. English is taught from the first year of schooling and, as we have seen, French and German are popular as third languages. The Norwegian language has a smaller vocabulary than English. As a result, Norwegians who use a literal translation when speaking English can lose the nuances of language and appear rather brusque.

CONVERSATION

In common with their fellow Scandinavians, Norwegians prefer to think before they speak. To an outsider, this can make conversation seem slow and a little stilted. It can be tempting to jump in with a barrage of questions to draw out your Norwegian friend, but try to resist. Personal questions, which a foreigner might regard as polite interest, will be viewed as rude and intrusive by a Norwegian. It is always best to keep the conversation light and general: sports, local places of interest, travel, and complimenting Norway are safe topics.

Because Norwegians think carefully about what they say, they are likely to have a serious expression on their face. This can also seem rather cold and off-putting, but is not intended to be so. They are merely giving careful consideration to the conversation. Remember too that the Norwegian may understand English better than they are able to speak it, so it may take them time to formulate their answer and, having done so, they might not word it in quite the way you expect. Hence, their response might seem very formal. Above all, do not rush in. Try to accept pauses as natural, give your Norwegian friend time, and let them lead the conversation.

Valuing honesty in others, Norwegians say what they mean and do not make casual remarks. This directness, coupled with little interest in small talk, can appear rather blunt to someone used to getting to the heart of the matter via the scenic route. Until you know someone well, you would probably be wise to avoid off-the-cuff involvements comments that you may intend to be amusing. In all likelihood your Norwegian friend will take you seriously and your comment will not receive the smile it deserves.

Norwegian straight talking means that in situations where the foreigner may expect a little sweetening of the pill, for example in dealing with the medical profession, then they are likely to be disappointed. Your doctor will be direct and to the point and is unlikely to have much of a "bedside manner."

BODY LANGUAGE

Norwegian reserve extends to body language. Norwegians are not effusive in their speech or their gestures. During conversation, they are likely to stand with their arms by their sides. Touching an arm or shoulder to make a point would not be acceptable. Like most Northern Europeans, they tend to stand a little further apart than their Southern counterparts. However, they are not obsessive about their own space and the people of the Stavanger area are often recognized by other Norwegians by how close they will stand to you in public places!

When engaged in conversation Norwegians maintain a serious expression with close eye contact, which foreigners can find a little unnerving. However, this is a courtesy on their part and shows that they are according you the respect of paying close attention to what you are saying. Eye contact is also an important aspect of the toasting ritual that accompanies a dinner. It is maintained while your fellows are wished *skål*.

If Norwegians nod when listening to you, it means merely that—that they are listening, not necessarily agreeing with you. The nod may be accompanied by a small "ah" sound, which is more like a sharp intake of breath. Again, it really just indicates that you are being listened to.

HUMOR

The rather "poker faced" expression that Norwegians seem to have while engaged in serious conversation can lead foreigners to believe that they have no sense of humor. This is quite wrong. In fact, Norwegians have a very dry sense of humor. Their economical use of words adds to the dryness of the wit, and telling jokes at the expense of their Swedish neighbors is something of a national pastime.

Have You Heard the One About . . . ?
A Swede called the airline and asked how long it would take for a plane to get from Stockholm to Paris. "Just a minute," said the clerk. "Thank you," replied the Swede, and hung up.

Q. Why do Swedes always drink their milk in the supermarket?
A. Because on the milk carton it says, "Open here."

Just to prove that the Norwegian sense of humor is alive and well, the town of Stavanger hosts the Great Norwegian Humor Festival each summer.

TV AND RADIO

In recent years Norway has seen an increase in the number of television channels available. In addition to the state-run NRK1 and NRK2, there are the commercial channels TV Norge and TV2. TV3 is a channel common to Norway, Sweden, and Denmark, although broadcast to each nation in its own language. It is also possible to pick up some other Scandinavian channels. Norway imports a large number of television programs from the U.K., U.S.A., and Australia. These are generally subtitled, not dubbed, so English-speaking viewers should have no difficulty finding something in English. Satellite and cable television are available in some areas.

The BBC World Service's English broadcasts can be received in Scandinavia, as well as output from the English-language NATO station.

NEWSPAPERS

Norwegians love their newspapers, and state advertising and government subsidies and loans ensure that 150 national and regional titles are published daily. Many have close links with political parties but there is no doubt that without generous subsidization a large number of the smaller papers would not be in production.

The big titles, based in the major towns, are largely independent. *Verdens Gang* claims the largest nationwide circulation figures, but *Dagbladet* and *Aftenposten* also attract high readerships. The *Bergens Tidende* and *Stavanger Aftenbladet* are two of the larger regional dailies. The principal business daily is *Dagens Næringsliv*. There are no English-language titles.

A wide range of weekly and monthly periodicals on all subjects is available in the Norwegian language. Newsdealers (the Narvesen chain predominates) in many of the larger towns sell a range of foreign newspapers and magazines.

TELEPHONES

Norway has one of the most advanced telecommunication networks in Europe. Its telephone system, operated by Telenor, is very reliable. Public telephones are widely available (deposit the money before making your call). They accept the full range of Norwegian coins: NKr1, 5, 10, and 20, although more and more are only taking phone cards, which can be purchased at Telehuser (Telenor shops), post offices, newsstands, stations, and some supermarkets. Most hotel rooms have phones, but these usually incur an unpleasantly large surcharge.

Norwegian telephone numbers always have eight digits, the first two of which are the area code. When Norwegians give you their telephone numbers they always speak in pairs of numbers. For example, they will give you the number 27558321 as twenty-seven, fifty-five, eighty-three, twenty-one. If they ask you for yours, try to give it in the same way.

To call Norway from outside the country, dial 00 47 followed by the eight digit number. To dial out of Norway, use the international access code 00 followed by the country code. Dial 117 for the operator, who will usually speak English.

Norwegians love the latest technology and almost all have a cell phone.

Useful Telephone Numbers	
International dialing code for Norway	00 47
Directory inquiries (Scandinavia)	180
Directory inquiries (international)	181
Operator (domestic calls)	115
Operator (international calls)	117
Police	112
Fire	110
Ambulance	113

MAIL

The opening hours of post offices vary slightly, but are usually within the 8:00/8:30 a.m. to 4:00/5:00 p.m. range Monday to Friday. Saturday hours are morning only. Some of the larger post offices in the main towns may offer slightly longer hours. Many close up to an hour earlier during the summer holiday period.

There are two rates for postage: A-post for priority mail, which is delivered the next day (except in the northern territories where it may take two days) and the cheaper B-post for economy. This takes longer and, in practice, tends to be used only for mass mailings. Mailboxes marked *inland* are for local domestic mail and *utland* for long distance and foreign post. The mail service is generally efficient, with mail to Europe taking two to four days and to the U.S.A. seven to ten days.

THE HIGH TECH NORWEGIAN

After centuries of living in remote valleys where communication with the next settlement was difficult for the simple reason that a mountain stood between, Norwegians have taken new technology to their hearts.

With one of the most advanced telecommunications networks in Europe,

telephones are at the center of the
communication revolution. The high
number of rural areas has also meant
that there is wide use of cellular mobile
systems instead of landline systems. Norway
was one of the first countries to take advantage of
the cell phone. Today the number of these in
circulation exceeds the number of Norwegians.

The benefit of the Internet was also quickly
realized. When the World Wide Web first spun its
way across the globe, Norway had more
computers per capita connected to the Internet
than any other country.

E-mail
Norway was one of the earliest countries to
embrace the Internet. E-mail is an excellent
means of communication in a country divided by
mountain and fjord. Today almost everyone will
have access to *e-post*.

Internet access is available in most hotels and
in the numerous cyber cafés found in the towns.
Many public libraries (*bibliotek*) also offer
plentiful Internet access.

CONCLUSION
Norwegians are fond of describing themselves as
simple people with simple tastes. Certainly it is

true that their deep respect for the natural world means that many of their pleasures are completely unsophisticated—walking in the mountains, swimming in the fjord, camping under the stars. However, in the twenty-first century they are highly educated members of a highly civilized— and highly successful—society.

Although a small nation, Norway is a force for moderation in the world, often acting quietly behind the scenes as a peace broker. It has used its oil windfall wisely to improve the lives of all Norwegians and to take the lead in generosity to poorer nations.

Repeatedly rated at the top of the United Nations index for the best country in the world to live, Norway provides a good social model to which many nations look when seeking to develop and improve their own societies. It derives comfort from its union with its fellow Scandinavian nations, but has the courage to stand alone when necessary.

Norwegians are fiercely patriotic, polite, generous, straight talking, and very hardy. The fact that most, particularly the young, speak English with such fluency can give the surface impression that getting to know them and all they stand for will indeed be simple. However, their natural reserve and the fact that they do not wear their hearts on their sleeves can soon make

them seem very complex to the foreigner new to
their shores.

In fact, time, patience and respect are the keys to
understanding the Norwegian people. Nordic
friendships are built on trust, sincerity, and honesty,
all of which take time to establish. Those prepared
to invest the time will find the reward of being
accepted a very warm and welcoming experience.

Further Reading

Brady, Michael, and Belinda Drabble. *Living in Norway: A Practical Guide.* Oslo: Palamedes Press, 2000.

Brimi, Arne. *A Taste of Norway.* Oslo: Norwegian University Press, 1987, 1990.

De Vries, André. *Live and Work in Scandinavia.* Oxford: Vacation Work, 1995, 2002.

Goth, Brian. *In the Desert of the Blue-Eyed Arabs: Cross-Cultural Management in the Norwegian Oil Industry from an Expatriate Perspective.* Working Paper 85/12. Oslo: Bedriftsokonomisk Institutt, Norwegian School of Management, 1985.

Lee, Phil, and Lone Mouritsen, James Procter, and Neil Roland. *The Rough Guide to Scandinavia.* London: Rough Guides, 2003.

Libaek, Ivar, and Øivind Stenerson (transl. Joan Fuglesang and Virginia Singer). *History of Norway: From the Ice Age to the Oil Age.* Oslo: Grøndahl og Dreyers Forlag AS, 1991, 1992.

Midgård, John. *A Brief History of Norway.* Oslo: Johan Grundt Tanum Forlag, 1963, 1971.

Roddis, Miles. *Norway (Lonely Planet Country and Regional Guides).* London: Lonely Planet Publications, 2005.

Slingsby, Cecil. *Norway: The Northern Playground.* Aberdeen: Ripping Yarns.com, 2003.

Streiffert, Anna, and Snorre Evensberget. *Norway.* Kent: Eyewitness Travel Guides, Dorling Kindersley, 2004.

Index

Acknowledgments

The author wishes to express her thanks to her husband, John March,
and to the staff of RC DEI as, Stavanger, Norway, for their invaluable
help and advice.